WOMEN IN SOCIETY

GERMANY

AGNES BOHNEN

MARSHALL CAVENDISH
New York • London • Sydney

Reference edition published 1993 by
Marshall Cavendish Corporation
2415 Jerusalem Avenue
P.O. Box 587
North Bellmore
New York 11710

© Times Editions Pte Ltd 1993

Originated and designed by
Times Books International, an imprint of
Times Editions Pte Ltd

Printed in Singapore

Library of Congress Cataloging-in-Publication Data:
Bohnen, Agnes,
    Women in society. Germany / Agnes Bohnen
    p. cm.—(Women In Society)
    Includes bibliographical references and index.
    Summary: Examines the experiences of women in German
    society, discussing their participation in various fields and
    profiling the lives of significant women.
    ISBN 1-85435-506-6
    1. Women—Germany—Social conditions—Juvenile
literature [1. Women—Germany. 2. Germany—Social
conditions.] I. Title. II. Series: Women in society (New York,
N.Y.)
HQ1623.B63 1992
305.42'0943—dc20   92–12375
                     CIP
                     AC

Women in Society

Editorial Director	Shirley Hew
Managing Editor	Shova Loh
Editors	Irene Toh
	Vijaya Radhakrishnan
	Goh Sui Noi
	Sue Sismondo
	Maureen Kelly
	Andrea Borch
	MaryLee Knowlton
Picture Editor	Yee May Kaung
Production	Edmund Lam
Design	Tuck Loong
	Ronn Yeo
	Felicia Wong
	Loo Chuan Ming
Illustrators	Jimmy Kang
	Kelvin Sim
MCC Editorial Director	Evelyn M. Fazio

Introduction

Germany is rich in traditions going far back in history, yet it is also modern and progressive, one of the leaders of Europe and the world. Balancing its two spirits, Germany reveals a kaleidoscope of attitudes that shapes German women of today. Traditional Germans think a woman's place is at home, but the 20th century winks and her roles are scattered somewhere between tradition and total liberation.

In this book, we review German women through two thousand years of history, starting from the days of the Roman empire. We open the door to two Germanies, to see how sisters divided by a wall grew up. East of this wall, women were discovering the conflict of being equal at work and alone at home, while west of the wall, the fight for work and equality went on. Perhaps this is what made Germany strong—the passion for perfection, discipline, and order that inspired one psychologist to comment, "German women are their own worst enemies, wanting to be perfect housewives and mothers, perfect lovers, and perfect career women."

We shall see that gypsies are also Germans and witness the heartaches and hopes of Turkish or Italian workers, and East European resettlers. Another Germany few have seen will appear, where teachers are put on trial by pupils and brides are still kidnapped on their wedding day. In this Germany, grandmothers no longer rock chairs but "around the clock." Through the lives of German women, we shall see some habits that are unmistakably "Deutsch."

Contents

Clara Schumann 7
Romance • The *Hausfrau* • Fulfilling a destiny • Career overboard

Milestones 11
Ancient Germans • Christianity • The Middle Ages • The 18th and 19th
centuries • The 20th century • Post-war Germany • The East German
experience • United Germany • What lies ahead?

Women in Society 37
Technical work • Business management • Law • Medicine • Politics •
Trade unions • Welfare • Media • Literature • Music and dance •
Movie production • Sports

Being Woman 67
The German resettlers • Minorities • German gypsies • Guest workers •
Moslems in a Christian land • Yugoslavian women • Italian women •
Greek women • Coming to terms

Profiles of Women 83
Ruth Pfau • Marie-Elisabeth Lueders • Helene Lange •
Louise Otto-Peters • Clara Zetkin • Johanna Kirchner •
Monika Griefahn • Marlene Dietrich

A Lifetime 103
Birth • Christian ceremonies • Teen years • Education •
Work • Marriage • Motherhood • Growing old

Women Firsts 124

Glossary 126

Further Reading 127

Index 127

chapter one

Clara Schumann

Her admirers included kings and empresses, and her storybook romance with composer Robert Schumann was material for many films. Pianist and composer Clara Schumann (1819–96) was a legend in her time and is still loved and admired. Though she lived and died a century ago, her story highlights aspects of German attitudes toward women that exist even today.

Clara was unusually talented and gave her first public concert at the age of 9. Her father, Frederick Wieck, a reputable piano teacher, dedicated his life to making her a piano virtuoso. When she was 13, he took her on her first European concert tour.

Romance

When Clara was just 11, Robert Schumann, 20, came to her father for piano lessons and lodging. They grew fond of each other over the years. By the time Clara was 16, the pair was deeply in love.

Frederick Wieck was furious as he had other plans for Clara. Why should his gifted daughter be, in his words, "an artist turned diaper washer, … a *Hausfrau* ("HOUSE-frao," meaning housewife) … tending porridge and infant wash?" He warned her about Robert's family history of insanity and even threatened to shoot Robert on sight. Clara submitted to his wishes. While she toured Europe, the heartbroken Robert tried to forget her. Later, however, the lovers met discreetly and, after a bitter court battle with Frederick Wieck, married in 1840.

Opposite: Clara Schumann.

Right: Robert Schumann, Clara's husband, was a German composer and music critic.

Clara Schumann was especially successful as a concert pianist. She was first to play Chopin's music in concert. In 1878 she was made the principal teacher of piano at Frankfurt Conservatory.

The Hausfrau

Their first home had two grand pianos in separate rooms. Clara lamented, "If only the partitions were not so thin." Though at the height of her career and more famous than Robert, she could hardly practice because he was studying and composing. When the first of their eight children came, Clara made sure Robert had the peace and quiet he needed to work, even as she despaired over her own curtailed career. During their marriage she managed to go on only three major concert tours—to Russia, Vienna, and Scandinavia. The one to Vienna was a flop because she had not practiced for months. For seven years she did not compose.

Robert sympathized but found it perfectly natural that she should be the one to sacrifice her career. Yet Clara needed her music. "I feel lighter and freer and everything seems happier and friendlier. The music is a great part of my life," she once said. "If it were missing, it would be as if all physical and mental elasticity had gone from me." Since Robert did not earn enough to support their family, she gave piano lessons and concerts.

Robert Schumann Five children to feed and no steady income induced Robert to take a job as music director in Duesseldorf in 1850. The sensitive and introverted composer was a disaster at the job. He was totally lost without Clara, yet when he accompanied her on concert tours, he became jealous and depressed because of her popularity. Though Clara reduced her own public appearances and helped him with his work, his depression deepened and he finally had to be admitted into a mental asylum where he died two years later, in 1956. Clara was only 37.

Johannes Brahms Another great composer, 14 years younger than Clara, Johannes Brahms, was inspired by her. He even babysat for her during one of her concert tours. Clara remained true to Robert, however, and allowed Johannes only a lasting friendship. He never married.

Fulfilling a destiny

Shortly after her husband was committed to an asylum, Clara started earning money as a concert pianist again. Her career gathered momentum after Robert's death and her children were left with different relatives, friends and tutors. From then on, her role as mother and homemaker faded and she gave in to her destiny to become once more the celebrated virtuoso.

Career overboard

It was very unusual in Clara Schumann's time for women to work, more so after they became mothers. Yet Clara, who broke many taboos, was revered as a motherhood idol. This was perhaps due not to her talent alone, but also to the sentimental image Germans had of her and her obvious need to support her family.

German women of the 20th century are more fortunate than Clara. Society still disapproves of working mothers, yet mothers returning to work after a "family pause" are increasingly common. Like Clara Schumann, most German women find greater fulfillment and happiness through work, but just like her they are prepared to shift their careers into lower gear when the children arrive.

The psycho-block

When she was 12, Clara composed her first song. At 15, she wrote her first opera. Considered the woman in the shadow of a genius, she wrote only 23 published compositions, many of which remain popular today. She lived in a time when society believed creativity was masculine and women could only play musical instruments, not compose. In reviewing one of her compositions, a critic wrote that the review was not to be considered a real "critique," because they were "dealing with the work of a lady." Of one of her compositions, Clara herself said, "Naturally it will always stay a woman's work, in which … strength and, here and there, creativity are missing." Prejudice could explain why she did not compose more.

Today, psychological barriers continue to divide jobs and behavior into "male" and "female." Fixed attitudes affect the styles and behavior of women in all walks of life. These attitudes not only influence the type of job women choose, but also the attitude of employers and society toward women. Women are banned from some jobs by law, while many employers are reluctant to hire girls for traditionally masculine work. Thus most girls today still choose typically "female" jobs and consequently have poorer job opportunities. German feminists have highlighted this fact, and in the last decade or so, the government and industrial sector have begun to listen and act.

Milestones

German history has been one of men's great deeds. Holding the fort at home while the men went to wars and crusades has become the traditional war-time role of women. In the chaotic aftermath, they were the repairers and renewers; women cleared up the debris, mothers gave birth to more sons to replace those lost at war, and wives comforted battle-worn husbands.

Time has not changed the roles, only the circumstances. Yet, when not restricted, German women have risen to glorious heights in politics, industry, the arts, religion, and science.

Ancient Germans

Germanic tribes moved south from countries like Sweden and Denmark more than 2,000 years ago. They were not very advanced, but had strict laws and a pagan religion with many gods. They were mainly shepherds and farmers, but these were turbulent times, when men would travel for years, warring and plundering, and the healing and nursing abilities of women meant the difference between life and death.

Opposite: German women have been the prime movers of their own fate, constantly calling and demonstrating for improvements.

Right: Ancient Germanic priestess.

Healing priestesses Among the women who followed warriors to battlefields were many skilled in minor surgery and first aid. Often, all they had were herbs, baths, compresses, and plasters. The only sicknesses these primitive people recognized were those arising from battle. Everything else was believed to be the work of evil spirits who had to be pacified or cast off by prayers, magical formulas, or blessings. Knowledge of healing and the role of priestesses were thus closely linked.

Priestesses were respected and obeyed. Military and political decisions hung in the balance as mighty warriors awaited the prophecies of these wise women. Barefoot and grey-haired, dressed in white gowns, bronze belts and fine flaxen cloaks, these women foresaw the future in blood flowing from prisoners' slit throats. One of the most famous priestesses was Veleda the Virgin. Her advice influenced decisions over war, peace, and alliances, and when battles were won, victory trophies were placed at her feet.

Wives and property At home, work was divided between the sexes. To the women went the housework; they spun, wove, and took care of the children, house, vegetable garden, poultry, and dairy farming. The men worked in the fields. When they went away to war, all their work fell to the women, too.

Despite her heavy responsibilities, the woman had few rights under tribal law. She was always under the guardianship of a male relative or her husband. Marriage was an economic decision made by the men of clans of equal wealth and standing. After the bridal price had been agreed upon, a woman (and later her children) became her husband's property—to be willed, sold,

or gambled away as he wished. Her dowry, her own property, was returned to her if she was sent away or widowed, but she had no say over its use. Property and inheritance were passed down the male line.

Chaste mothers of warriors In those rough and ruthless days, honor was upheld by men through blood-letting and other acts of vengeance, and sons were needed to increase tribal strength. A hero's lyric went, "A son is better, even if born late, after the master's departure …," for the souls of murdered fathers could rest in peace only if sons took blood revenge. If a woman did not bear sons, her husband could take as many concubines as he could afford.

Women were expected to be virtuous. There are many sagas of captured women of ancient Germany who killed themselves rather than lose their virtue. If a man had an affair with a married woman, he was said to have "trespassed on another man's property" and had to make compensation. The woman's mildest punishment was to have her long hair, a symbol of her honor, cut and to be chased naked from the village in front of the relatives. Some tribal laws called for the woman to be drowned or gruesomely killed.

So little were female lives valued that where there were too many, newborn baby girls were set out to die before

Thusnelda

Marriages were arranged by clans, but there were many love marriages through prearranged "kidnapping." The "kidnapped" woman lost her right to a dowry and other family gifts, but the marriage was usually accepted by her clan after her husband had paid a bridal price. Less acceptable were kidnap marriages when the bride was already engaged to someone else. A famous case was that of Thusnelda.

Thusnelda's father, a pro-Roman, refused to accept Arminius, a Cherusci tribal prince who had defeated the Romans. Arminius "kidnapped" her. Six years later, in A.D. 15, Thusnelda was recaptured and paraded through Rome with her son. She did not cry or beg for mercy, but stoically folded her arms and looked down at her pregnant body.

food had passed their lips. (It was Germanic custom that, once fed, a baby could not be abandoned.)

Tribal laws gave them few legal rights. But in practice, a Germanic woman's influence was great since she looked after the property. Historical accounts tell of the intelligence and organizational talent of Germanic women, as well as their courage in the face of danger. When their clan was attacked, Teutonic blondes with swords and axes rushed at invaders, wrenching shields from soldiers with naked hands, and fighting with blind courage to the death.

Great nuns

In the early days, the only literate women were nuns. Being well versed in science, literature, and the arts, nuns produced many books, encyclopedias, songs, and other works. Hrosvitha von Gandersheim (935–1000) was the first known German poetess. To give nuns an alternative to the frivolous comedies of Terence, a popular writer of the time, she wrote poems and six dramas in Latin. The dramas described the same vices and passion as in Terence's work, and with similar gusto, but had the saving grace of moral conclusions.

An abbess managed the convent (sometimes a monastery and a convent under one roof), its property, and wealth. She thus had wide powers. Under Otto I, abbesses were the only women on equal standing with bishops, abbots, and nobles. Many enjoyed great influence as kings and popes sought their advice. The church and the court allowed them more influence and status than were given to women outside the church.

One of the most famous nuns in history was the abbess Hildegard von Bingen (1098–1179). She was extraordinarily intelligent and talented, and she wrote in Latin about visions she had had from childhood. She produced numerous books, plays, music scores, and paintings. Hildegard von Bingen was also a healer and an authority on herbal medicine. Her book on medicine is valid even today.

Christianity

Around A.D. 500, Queen Clothilda talked her powerful husband, King Clovis of a Germanic tribe, the Franks, into converting to Christianity. Through that tender little nudge, most of Europe became Christian, for the religion was enforced in areas conquered by the Franks. Christianity deeply affected women's lives.

One man, one wife Christianity allowed a man only one wife, and she was no longer seen as property. This raised her status, though it took a few centuries for husbands to get used to monogamy.

Education Christianity also brought education to many women, even if the only aim was to teach them to read the Bible and religious books. (Women had always managed to find an outlet for learning and literature through religion when other forms were barred to them.) During the late Renaissance, a period of enlightenment that started in Italy around the 14th century, upper-class German women rose to great heights in the arts and literature. They became involved in church work and the education of girls.

In the Middle Ages, poor and destitute women and children found refuge in Beginen ("bay-GI-nen") homes founded and maintained by the church and rich people. Since there was no system of mass welfare, charitable work inspired by Christianity brought great relief. Women who had no outlet in work outside the home also found fulfillment in welfare work.

Marian cult Women were seen to be weak and sinful, like Eve, the original woman. A nun's life, filled with prayer and piety, became the ideal for women who wished to purify themselves from sin. Mary, mother of Jesus, was revered as a model of purity and the Marian cult affected the lives of women, who became deeply religious. It also led to the increase of nuns in the Middle Ages.

Convents At about the 10th century, a period of convent culture developed. Nuns and monks became known for their artistic and musical talents, and convents and monasteries were centers of learning. After the 13th century, a reform took away their cultural activities and enforced piety and asceticism. Convents lost their importance in learning and influence. However, they continued to be important as a refuge for women and illegitimate babies. Unwed mothers gave birth under a veil (to conceal their identity) in convents, and illegitimate babies were left at convent walls under cover of darkness. Convents saved thousands of babies from death.

Witches In contrast to nuns, other women were portrayed as inferior to men, punishable for Eve's original sin of tempting Adam with an apple. From the 13th to the 18th centuries, this view took a deadly turn in Germany, as it did in other parts of Europe. In a great inquisition, many women were tortured, hanged, or burned as witches and for allegedly working with the devil.

The trial of a witch. Women were tortured till they confessed to being witches.

Katarina von Bora

Many highly educated former nuns in Germany married Lutheran reformers and gave their husbands psychological support when the reform leaders came under criticism. By seeing to all the practical aspects of living, these women made it possible for the religious leaders to concentrate on their reforms.

Like his followers, Martin Luther generously refused payment for most of his lectures and books, so it was his wife, a former nun, Katarina von Bora (1499–1552), who fed the family and the numerous pilgrims and theologians who visited them. This she did by taking in paying lodgers, growing her own vegetables, and raising small animals.

Although most of Europe was Christian then, people still held pagan beliefs, blaming witchcraft and black magic for natural catastrophes like pests, droughts, and bad harvests. Since the church preached that women were the receptacles of sin, they became scapegoats. At the top of the list of suspects were midwives and women skilled in folk medicine. Although men were also accused, the majority of victims were women. In two villages, between 1587 and 1593, only two women were left alive.

Church reform The church was split into Catholic and Protestant after 1517 through the reform of a monk and theology professor, Martin Luther, who became the leader of the Protestant church. The ideal of the woman as a nun was replaced by her role as a mother. Martin Luther saw celibacy (the vow not to marry) as useless, so many nuns, monks and priests left their calling to marry. The status of wives and mothers was raised.

On the other hand, while more girls were taught, their education was limited to their roles as wives and mothers. When Martin Luther said, "Child upbringing and housekeeping: that is the vocation for which she was created by God" and "There is no skirt nor dress that suits a woman or virgin worse than when she tries to be clever," he was only saying what the rest of German society thought.

The Middle Ages

The Middle Ages were a feudal period when most peasants owned no property but worked and farmed for nobles in return for protection.

Aristocratic women Most noblewomen of the Middle Ages led sheltered lives confined to the castle and passed many hours every day reading religious books, spinning, or sewing. But with the men often away on battles or occupied with state matters, the lady of the manor managed property and so wielded great political power. One such noblewoman was Princess Gisela of Saxony, who also traveled extensively to look after her widespread property. She was described as the "mistress in the house, protectress and administrator of the property, servant and confidante of the Master, educator and teacher of the children."

Below: Empress Adelheid.

Royal glory

The influence of queens in the earlier period depended more on their personalities than on official power. Real power was conferred in the 10th century during the dynasty of Otto. In 960, when Otto I went to Rome, he left his mother, Mathilda, and the Archbishop of Mainz in charge of the kingdom. She was thus the first female head of government.

The second wife of Otto I, Adelheid (931–999), was crowned as Imperial Consort, making her an official ruler. In 962, she and Otto were crowned Empress and Emperor of the "Holy Roman Empire of the German Nation" by the pope. After the death of Otto I, she ruled for her son and, later, her grandson till they were ready to assume their duties.

Otto II's wife, Theophano, a Byzantine princess, was highly cultured and intelligent. After her husband's death, and with the help of Adelheid, she defended the throne for her 3-year-old son, Otto III. Theophano, a firm, confident, and glorious ruler, quelled the unrest caused by the struggle for the throne. She led the German troops herself to put down uprisings, to stabilize the eastern flanks of the empire, and to strengthen Italian ties. The mightiest of the empire bowed before her, and it was reported that "she united the entire empire under her command like a fetter."

Even queens and nuns spun and did needlework. Luitgardis, the daughter of Otto the Great, was so famed for her spinning that a golden spindle was put up at her grave. Women wore spindles at their waist, and law books talked of the allowance made to girls and women as "spindle money." A social event for all classes would be an evening together spent spinning.

A mistress and her maid spinning thread.

Feudal peasants About 90% of the population were peasants. Some were free, but many were bonded to the king and nobles, the church, convents, and monasteries. They were given protection and in return paid taxes in kind, providing labor or farm produce such as eggs, meat, wool, and linen. For the women this might mean washing, making clothes, tending the vegetable garden, baking, or preparing beer—in addition to working on land leased to

them and doing the very same chores for their own families.

In the 8th century, Charlemagne introduced new varieties of fruits and vegetables as well as food preservation methods like salting and smoking meat. It improved the food situation but added to women's work. They also had to make clothes for everyone, including the farmhands. In those times, everything had to be made from scratch: preparing the flax, spinning thread, weaving cloth, and sewing clothes by hand. Farm women were often worn out or died young, and were soon replaced, for no farmer could manage without a wife.

Rural maids War and disease left more women than men. Since the church preached celibacy and monks and priests could not marry, and often only master craftsmen were allowed wives, many women remained single and had to support themselves. They worked in trades and crafts; for noblemen, in fields, houses, and animal sheds; or in the *Frauenhaus* ("FRAO-'n'-house," meaning the House of Women), making cloth and clothes. There were no regulations for working hours or conditions, so maids were a terribly exploited class.

Women's guilds In the 13th century, women could become independent by joining guilds. Some were master craftswomen who trained apprentices

and hired helpers. At first the only rule was that master craftswomen, like master craftsmen, had to be able to work physically in the trade. Thus they were weavers, makers of bedding, butchers, bakers, smiths, and merchants of chickens, eggs, fruit or general goods. Jobs like gold-spinning and thread-making became their special field.

Even prostitutes formed guilds and were acknowledged by the church and town, for their taxes were a good source of income. Female troopers were also organized in guilds. They cleaned camps, filled up trenches, and helped position cannons in battle. They also served male troopers by cooking, sweeping, cleaning, washing, nursing, and bringing food to the battlefield.

In large towns, women were not allowed to sign contracts, do business, or go to court without their husbands' consent, but businesswomen could do all these activities. Later, in some towns, women were excluded in certain circumstances. In Cologne, they were not allowed to make men's clothes. Elsewhere, heavy work was forbidden eventually. Some widows were permitted to take over their late husbands' trade while others had to sell out. At times, a widow could choose a worker from her dead husband's guild to marry and run the business.

Workers were regulated long before unions were thought of, and even fish sellers in a market had to belong to a guild. (Painting by Lorenzo Quaglio)

Housewives and mothers In hard times and also because of competition from cheaper rural craftsmen, town master craftsmen and workers could not earn enough to feed their families. At the same time, the church reinforced the role of women as housewives and mothers whose priorities were husband, children, and kitchen.

Everyone helps in this home factory: a boy cuts logs into short lengths while other family members carve them into miniature horses and a girl amuses her baby sister.

By the 17th century, independent tradeswomen were banned from many trades, and they were not allowed to join guilds. Their only recourse was to work within a family business run by their husbands or fathers.

The extended family The households of farmers, skilled workers, and tradesmen were mini-factories. Depending on the size of the enterprise, everyone, including unmarried aunts, children, apprentices, or maids, helped in the production, sale, and administration of the product. The father represented the extended family in public, especially when women were not allowed in guilds.

The wife had important economic functions. She held the purse strings because she sold the finished products, bought raw materials, kept the books, and was an expert in quality, commercial law, and customer service. She also taught and fed the workers, did the housework, and looked after the children.

As if that was not enough, the wife also prepared or made everything the family needed—from meals, soap, candles, clothes, and shoes, to bedding, beer, and ink. For the woman, gainful employment, family, and household were integrated.

Her circumstances did not change until the Industrial Revolution of the 18th century.

The 18th and 19th centuries

The French Revolution (1789–1815) that swept away feudalism in France did not spread to Germany, its only echo there being some uprisings and reforms. The greatest effects were in literature and intellectual activity. This was the age of some of Germany's greatest writers like Goethe and Schiller, and philosophers like Hegel and Kant.

Literary salons

When liberal ideas were spreading in Europe in the latter half of the 18th century, a small circle of educated Berlin women became famous for their literary salons.

The salons (living rooms) were centers where men and women met to exchange ideas and discuss current issues. It was a time when conversation and letter-writing were important forms of communication and entertainment. A salon was one of the rare places women could go to, without being escorted by a man, for mental stimulation outside the home.

One of the most respected and fascinating of these women was a Jew, Rahel Varnhagen von Ense (1771–1833). Despite being mostly self-educated, she was a brilliant and impressive conversationalist. Jews were not welcome in the homes of Prussian high society in her time, but at 20, Rahel managed to gather aristocrats, diplomats, states-men, writers, artists, and professors in her salon, a small, sparsely furnished attic room where she served biscuits or sandwiches, tea and roasted chestnuts.

Rahel was a prolific writer of letters and diaries that her 14-year-younger husband, Karl August Varnhagen, collected and had published after her death. When Rahel was 57, the Austrian dramatist, Grillparzer, said of her, "She ... began to speak and I was spellbound ... She spoke and spoke till midnight and I don't remember: did they chase me off or did I go myself? I have never in my life heard any more interesting and better conversation."

The Industrial Revolution Gradual but far-reaching changes came through the Industrial Revolution that began in the late 18th century. Large-scale machinery was used for mass production, and manufacturing moved away from the home to the factory. The work place and the home were separated.

Wives and daughters of tradesmen lost their economic role with the disappearance of the family enterprise. From being producers, they became consumers, and their husbands were no longer independent businessmen but employees.

Family life grew in importance as a refuge for men from the anxieties of working life, and many people longed for the old days.

Working women joined factory lines during the Industrial Revolution.

Middle-class lifestyle During the Industrial Revolution, the opening of banks and new businesses led to the rise of a class of newly rich who tried to copy the aristocratic lifestyle. Women of this class despised work, the pride of generations of German housewives. At the same time, in the second half of the 19th century, education was seen as unfeminine. Well-brought-up women knew as little as possible about the real world.

Marriage meant lifelong social security, and married women enjoyed a high status. Unfortunately, more than 50% of middle-class women could not marry because there was a shortage of men, and the dowry their families had to bring to the marriage was prohibitive. Even lower middle-class women considered paid work and job training a disgrace. In many families that could not make ends meet, daughters and wives sewed secretly by night and pretended to be idle or to do fine needlecraft by day. Housemaids, a status symbol, were musts even if the family had to starve to keep them.

The emancipators A revolution in France in 1848 led to uprisings in Germany and revolts against the rulers. Women like Louise Otto-Peters (see Chapter 5), Fanny Lewald, Lily Braun, and others began to write about social injustice and their own social position.

Women still could not sign documents or practice a profession without their husbands' permission. They had no rights over their own earnings, and they could not vote.

The education of girls was of a very low standard. Its aims, as stated in a teachers' conference of 1872, were "… in order that the German husband should not be bored at the domestic hearth by the intellectual short-sightedness and narrow-mindedness of his wife and thereby cripple his dedication to higher interests."

Middle-class women's association In 1865, the General German Women's Association was founded with Louise Otto-Peters as its president. Its leaders

Hedwig Dohm (1833–1919) was one of the first to call for the right of women to vote. She demanded equality for men and women in private and public law and in education. "Human rights have no sex," she declared, but she stood alone. Even the organized women's movement found her too provocative.

Lily Braun (1865–1916), one of the moderate members of the Working Women's Association. She wrote many books on the social circumstances of the time and was the first to develop the idea of motherhood insurance for working women.

realized they could only improve women's circumstances through work and better education. The long fight for equal education and university studies was led by Helene Lange (see Chapter 5), and women were finally admitted

Rosa Luxemburg

One of the most colorful members of the socialist movement in Germany was the Polish-born Jew and revolutionary, Rosa Luxemburg (1871–1919). When she was 19, Red Rosa, as she was known, fled from Russian police who wanted her because of her resistance activities. In Switzerland she studied political science, law, and economics and met many Polish revolutionaries, among them Leo Jogisches, who became her friend and lover. She was one of the founders of the secret Social Democratic Party of Poland.

Believing that social revolution would take place in Germany, she entered a marriage of convenience to get German citizenship. She joined the Social Democratic Party in Germany and became one of Germany's first independent women politicians.

Rosa was a fiery and brilliant orator and theoretician, and she had great charisma. She was imprisoned many times in Germany and Poland for her anti-war and revolutionary activities, as well as for agitating for revolution of the masses through strikes. A strong believer in democracy, she criticized Lenin, the Russian socialist leader, for his despotic one-party rule and reign of terror. "The proletarian revolution needs no terrorism to achieve its aims; it hates and abhors the murder of its fellowmen," she said.

Rosa Luxemburg often fought with her own party over ideological differences and eventually broke away to form the Communist Party of Germany with Clara Zetkin and Karl Liebknecht, a lawyer. Yet, in spite of her uncompromising attitude and sharp political attacks, she was a tender-hearted and humane woman with a love for literature and nature. Her great influence on radical socialists has survived decades after her brutal murder in 1919. When the East Germans were demonstrating against their government in 1989, they repeated Rosa Luxemburg's words: "Freedom is the freedom of those who hold a different opinion."

into colleges in 1901. These courageous women were ridiculed, yet clearly they threatened male dominance. Laws were passed at this time to stop women from becoming editors and to ban them from political associations.

The General German Women's Association tried only to give women better chances in work and education. Except for a radical wing, it did not fight for women's right to vote till 1917. Through taking a moderate course, however, it spread the women's movement. In 1894, the Federation of German Women's Associations was founded as an umbrella organization.

The working class The problems of working women were different from those of the middle class. They did not have to fight for the right to work. They *had* work—too much of it, for starvation wages, and under terrible conditions. In towns, workers in textile factories were lower-class country girls or the wives and daughters of workers, craftsmen, and low-ranking civil servants. The cost of living in towns was high, and women tried to help out by selling garden vegetables or rabbits. Housewives took in pre-cut material to sew at home. The spread of home sewing machines contributed greatly to the home industry. Yet, even though the family could not survive without the help of working wives and daughters, their earnings were dismissed as merely "pocket money." This attitude led to longer hours for increasingly less pay for working women.

A working-class women's movement was begun by Gertrude Guillaume-Schack and taken over by Clara Zetkin (see Chapter 5). It fought for better working conditions, better pay, and the protection of mothers from excessive work. Unlike the middle-class General German Women's Association, it also fought for political rights. Eventually, it broke away from the other association.

The Working Women's Association was part of a larger movement, the socialist movement, which fought for a society where everyone was equal through state ownership of production. Some leaders of the movement believed change would come through reform. Others demanded revolution. Many branches of the Working Women's Association were founded, as well as trade unions. Women could not legally participate in politics, so they constantly clashed with the police.

Ironically, the Working Women's Association had to fight with male members of the larger socialist movement, who wanted to remove women as competitors in the work place. August Bebel, Social Democratic Party leader, argued on the side of women in his book, *Woman and Socialism*. Under his influence the union fought for women for the first time.

The 20th century

For a short time after World War I (1914–18), women surged into public life. During the war, they had slipped into the jobs of men called up for military service and had proved capable. Many women had also lost their husbands and had to work for a living.

Above: Women lining up for food and other essentials after World War I.

Opposite, top: Sophie Scholl.

Opposite, bottom: Federation of German Girls member in uniform.

Women got the right to vote in 1918, when Germany became a republic. Among the pioneering politicians were determined women like Marie-Elisabeth Lueders (see Chapter 5), whose energy helped introduce important laws for women and children.

Return to the hearth Then came the economic depression after World War I, and with it widespread unemployment. Women were once more seen as competition to bread-earning men. Women doctors and other women holding high posts were forced out of their jobs.

In 1923, married women were banned from the civil service, and many pregnant women were dismissed to save on medical insurance. They returned to their traditional duties, searching for bread, coal, and meat. Women leaders concentrated on social welfare and left foreign affairs, economics, and financial policies to the men.

Nazis and mothers Something worse was to come. The Nationalist Socialist German Worker's Party (NSDAP or NAZI party) rose to power in 1930. Its leader, Adolf Hitler, took advantage of the chaotic political situation, spiralling inflation, and massive unemployment and used mass propaganda and violence to gain control. In 1933, he became the Fuehrer (leader) and soon led Germany into another war. His rule was the worst era of modern Germany when millions of Jews, gypsies, people with disabilities, and others were murdered.

In 1932, 6 million Germans were unemployed. Part of the policy to fight unemployment was to proclaim that a "Woman's Place Is In The Home," and to support this, the number of female college students was limited to 10%. Motherhood became a national duty, and bronze, silver, and gold merit medals were actually awarded to mothers of many children. Interest-free loans were

Sophie Scholl

In World War II, many German women worked with the Nazis, some of them in concentration camps. They could be as cruel as the men. But there were also men and women who resisted the Nazis when even a hint of criticism meant death. Many did so passively by not cooperating. Women with children used prams to hide anti-Nazi leaflets, and others played innocent housewives by day and typed resistance propaganda on sound-absorbing mattresses at night.

Among the young resistance fighters were those of the White Rose group, of which Sophie Scholl (1921–43), an undergraduate, was a member. Together with her brother and friends, she distributed leaflets in the college in Munich calling for resistance and condemning Hitler's policies. They were arrested and during their trial, she declared, "If my brother has been condemned to death, then I may not get a milder sentence because I am just as guilty as he." Their executors reported that they went to their deaths "without blinking an eye." They fought against suppression and brutality although the fight was as good as hopeless from the start. But through their actions, the resistance members gave others hope that there would be another Germany.

offered to newlyweds, especially if the bride gave up her job.

Girls joined the Federation of German Girls, the work service, or the "NS Frauenschaft" for women—organizations to serve the people and prepare girls for their future womanly roles. The NS woman leader, Scholtz-Klink, said in 1934, "The woman must be such that she does everything that is asked of her gladly."

In 1932, the Federation of Women's Associations folded up rather than be absorbed into Nazi organizations, and some of its leaders emigrated or joined the resistance movement. The remaining women's organizations lost their independence and concentrated on cooking, motherhood, bridal and handicraft classes, and charity work. Just before war broke out in 1938, because of the labor shortage, women under 25 had to work for one year on farms or in households before taking their first job. As war took the men away, more and more women took over their jobs.

"Rubble Women"

After World War II, large groups of women cleared the debris of bombed-out Germany. Using bare hands and shovels, they cleaned streets and sorted bricks to repair houses, saving millions from freezing. This reserve army was often paid only a small "rubble fee" and a bowl of hot gulash soup. Some had been through two world wars and brought up children singlehandedly. When their husbands returned, often war-damaged, they complained of being faced with "rubble removal" and "reconstruction work" at home to boot.

"Rubble Women" refers also to a whole generation who helped rebuild Germany, preventing the country from breaking down. In spite of laws protecting women from heavy and dangerous work, German women worked in mines, iron, metal and machinery factories, cement works, and construction sites. They looked for heavy work as it paid an extra allowance and that meant more food for the family.

Post-war Germany

In May 1949, Germany was divided into East and West, with the Russians occupying the eastern sector and the Americans, British, and French the western sector. For four decades thereafter, Germans lived under two systems: communism (east) and democracy (west).

America lends a hand After the war, the Americans brought ideas of democracy to the Germans. They organized conferences and workshops and brought together groups of women. A "Persons Exchange Program" gave many German women the chance to learn the American way of life firsthand. The Americans also helped set up and finance an information service. This was important because the experience of collaboration under Hitler had left Germans with a bad aftertaste; through the new information service, associations could keep in touch without losing their independence.

The German Women's Council Out of these beginnings, the German Women's Council was founded as the umbrella organization for about 80 associations. Throughout the broad spectrum of its members—11 million women—it is the mouthpiece for women in Germany. Today the organization acts as a consultant to the government and political organizations and does valuable pre-parliamentary work.

The new women's movement In the recession that followed World War II, the two largest political parties formed a coalition government. An organized opposition, the Federation of Socialist German Students, whose members questioned the old social order, grew outside parliament. It formed an Action Council for the Freedom of Women to demand new methods of child care and a new relationship between men and women.

Ironically, the activities of the Federation mirrored the very ills of the society it opposed. The men led discussions and demonstrations; they planned the campaigns. The women were asked to type, make coffee, and look after the participants' children; they had hardly any influence. Helke Sanders, one of the leaders, led an appeal for change in 1968, which brought no positive response from the men. After throwing a few well-placed tomatoes at their male colleagues during a heated debate, the women broke away.

The new women's movement was part of a larger movement coming from America, through France and Holland. Women of many different backgrounds were searching for a new identity. Rejecting the old feminism, they tried to change the social situation by using self-therapy and increasing the awareness of women. Their activities ranged from studies of, among other subjects, Marxism, and sexuality and a new motherliness, to female mysticism. An entire Female Culture grew, with women-only cafés, clubs, and bookshops; feminist literature, theater, and films; cabarets, dance, and music evenings without men; and newspapers for women. Small groups met in private or public rooms. Later, Women Centers sprang up in many towns and grew into a dense network.

Suspicious of tradition and hierarchy, the new movement had no umbrella organization. Its aims were varied. Through one issue, however, its members were unified: a spectacular demonstration against the abortion laws initiated by a journalist, Alice Schwarzer. In an action copied from France, 374 women admitted, "I have had an abortion."

Alice Schwarzer (second from right), one of the leaders of the modern women's movement. Her magazine, *Emma*, exposed violence against women, incest, and pornography, hitherto taboo topics.

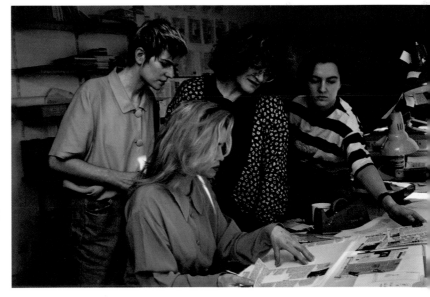

Above: The anti-abortion laws demonstration in 1971.

At first, there were large differences between the old and new movements. The old movement worked within the existing framework, that is, the women participated in existing institutions and were close to the centers of power. The new movement preferred to work within its own political party. Later, realizing the need for unity, the movements worked more closely together.

Legal milestones

Equal before the law   Elisabeth Selbert (below) proposed a motion to change the constitution, giving women equal legal rights with men. The "Four Mothers of Constitution" (Elisabeth Selbert, Helen Wesel, Helene Weber and Friederike Nadig) organized women into a massive protest action. Trade unions, women's associations, and female politicians and journalists demonstrated in support of the motion.

The law was to take effect in 1953 but only did so in 1958. Women finally had rights over their own property, the "final decision" authority of the husband in marital matters was revoked, and decisions on children's upbringing rested with both parents instead of just the father.

Citizenship   In 1972, children of German women married to foreigners could be German citizens, no matter where they were born. Previously this ruling applied only to children of German men with foreign wives.

The right to a job   In 1977, husbands could no longer have their wives dismissed from jobs. This ended a law that gave a woman the right to work only if working did not interfere with her duties to her marriage and family. This law had forced her to give up her job to be a housewife if her husband demanded it.

Equal in the work place   In 1980, the law on equality of men and women in the work place was passed. It included the issue of equal pay for equal work. In the civil service, equal pay for equal work is now a reality.

Child-care leave and subsidy   In 1986, child-upbringing leave was introduced in recognition of women's calls for help in balancing work and family. Mothers were paid 600 Deutschmarks (about $375) monthly for 18 months. Fathers, too, are eligible.

Pension for "Rubble Women"   From October 1, 1987, in recognition of their contribution during and after World War II, women born before 1921 were given an increased monthly pension of 28 Deutschmarks (about $18) for every child born alive.

Quotas   In the 1980s, a major milestone was achieved when quotas for women gained support. In the government service and many welfare organizations, if two equally qualified people apply for a job, a female applicant is selected till women hold half the jobs in the department.

Recent legal milestones   Women are now allowed to keep their maiden names after marriage. In the spring of 1992, the ban on night work for women workers was lifted.

East German agricultural women workers.

The East German experience

In theory, a socialist system allows men and women to be equal. The socialist government of East Germany believed the inequality of women could be reduced by changing the law and giving women work, thus making them less dependent on men.

When the Russians took over the eastern part of Germany after World War II, East Germany, like its counterpart in the west, was very short on men and material and women's labor was needed. In 1946, women were given equal pay for equal work. In 1949, the constitution pronounced men and women equal. Since the state dictated the occupation of each citizen according to the country's needs, women worked in all kinds of jobs, including typically male ones like mining, construction, and engineering. In agriculture, women worked as hard as men and underwent the same training.

Girls studied medicine, science, and technical subjects. The unskilled were sent for courses. Women were given every possible financial, moral, and practical help to upgrade their education and training. As a result, in the 1950s, more than 90% of women between 15 and 60 were either working or in job training, 60% had a professional qualification and 25% a college education.

Motherhood incentives and choices To increase the birth rate, women were given financial and other incentives, including a paid "mother's year," shorter working weeks, and longer annual leave. Undergraduates with babies had state support, including postponement of examinations, baby care, kindergartens, and financial help.

Women could also opt for abortion within 12 weeks of pregnancy, and birth control pills were free of charge, so that childbearing became planned.

Balancing act Women were still given two official roles: that of a man at work and that of a mother and housewife at home. The government tried to lighten their burden by providing a vast network of childcare centers to care for children, supervise their homework, and feed them lunch, while work brigades helped with housework, including ironing and sewing.

But the East Germans lacked modern household aids. In addition, the chronic shortage of supplies meant long hours in lines for even essentials like clothes and fruit.

Husbands were supposed to help with household chores and the children by law, and a woman could sue for divorce if her husband neglected to help at home. In practice, the women were left with most of the work and felt guilty about leaving their children in a child-care center or alone at home. They were also being chased from Marxism to management courses in the craze for qualification.

Overburdened East German women compared themselves with the state ideal of a woman balancing work, children, and politics—and found themselves wanting. Since there was no free media and no women's movement to focus on the real situation, these women thought their failure was a personal one rather than an inevitable, collective problem. One result of the social conflict was the high rate of divorce (higher than 36%) and the number of single mothers (about 33% of mothers).

Finally, East German women lowered their ideals, and many went into jobs requiring lower qualifications. This prompted the leaders to say it was not worth promoting women because they always dropped out for family reasons. From the 1970s, East German women started to be channeled back into stereo-typed "female" jobs. Later, the men were given a 50% quota in colleges, and college places in some fields of study were reserved for them.

A changing state portrait The official picture of an East German woman in the media did not reflect the reality but the economic and ideological needs of the country. At the end of the 1950s, the media showed a self-assured working woman. In the 1960s, the highly qualified and well-educated career woman was portrayed. Children and household were very much hidden in the background, and young student mothers were frowned upon.

When the population figures dropped, the picture changed. Now the mother of three children, the successful career woman, and the politically engaged citizen balancing all three jobs efficiently was the official ideal. People married young since new housing was given only to married couples.

In the 1980s, when questions of women in top posts were raised, the government's excuse was that it would be unfair to women to expect them to sacrifice more time and effort, especially as they were already burdened with children and their households. Finally, although they were promised equal pay and held middle and upper manage-ment posts, a survey in 1988 showed that women earned 78% of what men earned.

Women's organizations Since officially women were emancipated, there was no need for a women's movement; none was tolerated. Unlike in West Germany, where the women's movement was splintered into many groups, the only official women's association in East Germany was the Democratic Federa-tion of Women in Germany, founded in 1945. This was an extension of the state organ. While it helped to improve some of the women's practical problems and organized work brigades and cultural and political education, the Federation's main job was to explain and gain support for state policies.

In the 1980s, the beginnings of a women's movement appeared when women first protested against the military service law of 1972 that allowed women aged 18 to 50 to be drafted as an expression of equality.

In 1989, thousands of East Germans started to find refuge in West German embassies in East European countries. Women participated in all the demonstrations against the communist regime in East Germany in the days before its downfall in the fall of 1989.

The Democratic Federation of Women was reorganized and is now working with the German Women's Council.

United Germany

Germany was united in 1990. East Germany is now called the New Federal States and West Germany the Old Federal States. The unity that had been longed for by both sides has meant sacrifices, too, more so from the East Germans. Antiquated factories in the east have closed. Jobs have been lost, as well as old socialist privileges like child-care centers and guaranteed jobs. East Germans are learning to live in democracy and capitalism, as well as freedom from the fear of the secret police. Many still need to adjust to the market economy.

Looking beyond the chaos, the benefits are clear. The New Federal States bring a huge reservoir of highly trained and educated personnel to a united Germany. Women have known privileges that their sisters in the Old Federal States are still fighting for. Their political awareness adds to the strength of the women's lobby.

What lies ahead?

The history of German women has been one of repeated suppression, but the last decade has shown more understanding and redress. While there are always new setbacks to overcome, women have taken on broader roles. Greater women's participation in society has become the norm, partly because of a steady economy.

Two women chip away at the wall that divided two Germanies.

But history teaches how milestones can quickly turn into tombstones. A new anti-feminist mood is gathering momentum. German women can safeguard their position not just through competence and qualification, but also through giving other women a helping hand.

Female solidarity, however, does not mean being anti-men. Competition calls for aggression, but cooperation brings mutual help and benefit. In Germany, the key word describing the desired relationship between men and women in the coming decade is "partnership."

chapter three

Women in Society

The 1980s and early 1990s have brought women far-reaching changes in almost all walks of life. History has not been kind to women in Germany, but a strong economy, equal educational opportunities, the international focus on women, as well as the determined pressure of women's groups and new attitudes, have powered change and progress.

Real gains have been made in the job sector as government and businesses are trying to give women better opportunities. Now more than ever, women are making their presence felt. In this chapter, we look at the accomplishments of women in many fields of endeavor and see how they share a common quality—an unrelenting determination to succeed.

Technical work

Female faces behind grease smears may still turn a few heads, but they are no longer unthinkable. Still, many employers hesitate to hire women for technical jobs, even though pilot projects have proven women are just as competent with wrenches and drills as men. Women leaders have pointed out that industry cannot afford to be rigid in its attitudes toward hiring women as they are becoming more qualified. In the New Federal States (formerly East Germany), there are many more technically skilled women than in the Old Federal States (formerly West Germany) because of their earlier policies of putting women into all job sectors.

Opposite and right: Being a mechanic and an atomic research worker are just two of a multitude of job options open to women today.

Campaigns Pilot projects and campaigns with upbeat posters like "Laser and Lipsticks" have been launched by the West German government and trade associations since the 1970s. They were designed to interest girls in technical jobs. The target was also employers, parents, teachers, and friends, who influence girls' job choices.

The campaigns have borne fruit. Today, many technical companies try to attract girls by organizing Open Days, Family Days, and Girls and "Technic" Days. To provide girls with greater social identification with technical work, some companies use female trainers, highlight past role models in technical fields, and give them technical projects related to the woman's world.

Attracting and training women are all very well, but what then? They need jobs in their trained fields. In large concerns, more women are getting these opportunities and the number of female apprentices in technical fields has tripled. While most of the women with master certificates in a trade are in typical female branches like body care, hairdressing or textiles, increasing numbers have been qualifying in technical, wood and building and machinery construction, computers and electronics, and other trades.

Banned In the Old Federal States, women, especially those of childbearing age, are still restricted or banned from some jobs. This is to protect them from

From housewife to master

Franziska Firch, who started as a housewife soldering in the Siemens company in Augsburg, qualified as a signal communication mechanic. She is also an Industrial Electronics Master. It took years of part-time study; her son often commented, "Homework again?" and soon learned to be independent. At first in charge of a department of 129 people producing keyboards and monitors, Franziska is now heading a department of 60 for customized software programs.

extremely heavy work, exposure to dangerous situations, radiation, and toxic chemicals, such as may be found in mines, at construction sites or in blast furnaces. Some of these restrictions have been lifted in some states in recent years, but others remain.

Certain trade associations limit women apprentices to daughters of craftsmen taking over the family enterprise. Others admit those who need to learn the trade as "practicals" for architectural, engineering, or other technical studies but do not allow them to practice the trade. Some associations tolerate the existence of craftswomen who work without being registered in the trade chambers, as long as no one complains officially. Many women want to have the right to make their own decisions. Some have fought in court for their right to work in banned fields and won.

There are now training centers for women in trades, such as the House of Craftswomen in Cologne and Berlin. Through moral and concrete support and practical courses, the centers hope to encourage more girls into trades.

German women, say psychologists, are their own worst enemies. They want to be perfect housewives and mothers, perfect lovers, perfect career women.

Business management

Engineering, science, mathematics, law, business studies, and economics are the subjects career-oriented German women study. Career women of the past generation say they did not plan their careers; they just took opportunities that arose. Younger women, however, know where they want to land by the time they are 30. Their ambitions may change boardroom faces in coming decades.

Women are in a minority—7.8%—in middle management positions. Even fewer—5.9%—reach the very top, and German women still lag behind the American, French, and Italian women in management. Yet progress has been made. In banking, for example, the ratio of male to female managers used to be 20 to 1; now it is 12 to 1, and it is improving.

Women managers are more likely to be found in personnel and accounting departments. Fewer are seen in sales and marketing, where star careers are nurtured, or in production, and research and development.

Boardrooms and token women "Group photo with a lady" has been used to describe the situation at the top where women in boardrooms are still rarities. Although many of them are highly qualified, women who make it to the top are often suspected of being token or "alibi" women, given the post by

Dual career families

In Germany where, it was said, husbands take better care of their cars than their wives and women choose cars by their color, Dr. Erica Emmerich seems an unlikely choice as president of the Association of German Motor Vehicles Manufacturers, with 400 members and 750,000 employees. Up to 1988 the president of Federal Motor Vehicle Authority in Flensburg, she was the first woman to head a technically oriented federal agency. At the same time, she was active politically as a Christian Democratic Union party member and brought up three daughters singlehandedly after her divorce in 1979. Her daughters assure her they have not suffered from having an active mother. Success was a matter of time, organization, and great discipline.

Family and lack of childcare facilities are tripwires for career women, whether employees or entrepreneurs. "A 14-hour day [for the mother] is asking too much of a child," said one entrepreneur to *Der Spiegel* magazine. Many successful German women are unmarried, divorced, or childless. Successful German men, on the other hand, are mostly married fathers. Determined women combine both family and career, ignoring society's disapproval of working mothers and hiring domestic help or roping in husbands for chores. This trend toward dual career families is encouraged by the publicity given to successful career women with supportive husbands.

Men who work late are considered ambitious. Women who do the same are called "raven mothers," a derogatory term implying neglect of their children. Women managers have had to become more efficient; meetings are shorter and work gets done faster because a second shift is waiting for them back home. They are also generally more cooperative and team-oriented, qualities recognized as the new management style.

companies or politicians who want to improve their image or win women's votes. Top banker Ellen Schneider-Lenné, the first woman executive board director in Deutsche Bank and on the board of the chemical firm ICI in England, disagrees. "Women don't have to be mollycoddled. They are every bit as good as men and simply have to compete on the same basis," she says.

Entrepreneurs The very idea of entrepreneurship is contagious, and women are catching the business bug. One out of three new businesses is in female hands. "The unsuccessful career woman in a male-oriented branch is the successful woman entrepreneur," says Hamburg lawyer Helga Stoedter. Some enter the field because they want flexibility in balancing family and career.

Two entrepreneurs

Jil Sander, fashion designer

Frustration at not getting her ideas past some editors made an entrepreneur out of the then 24-year-old fashion writer Heidemarie Jiline Sander in 1967. Today, with annual sales of $200 million, her company owns one of the best known labels of exquisite fashions made in Germany.

Her first collections brought sweet success with a bitter edge. She was deluged with orders she could not deliver. The first three years, 1973–76, saw insolvent customers, problems caused by inexperience, strikes, and production hitches in Italy. Her first two attempts in Paris failed, but at Milan in Italy, in 1988, she scored a huge success. The company expanded, adding cosmetics and eyewear products to clothes. In 1989, shares of her company were floated on the stock market, making it the only public enterprise headed by a woman in Germany.

Elisabeth Noelle-Neumann, journalist and professor

Knowledge means money, whether it involves saving billions of dollars through making the right investment, or commercial success through knowing how to meet customer needs. Professor Dr. Noelle-Neumann (born 1917) has made it her business to know what the nation thinks. At Allensbach, she runs an institute for opinion research. She founded it with her journalist husband in 1946, after a student exchange year in the United States where she learned the Gallup method of opinion research. Now, the professor is an international expert on the subject and lectures at several universities around the world.

She advises the federal chancellor (Germany's head of state), and her clients include government departments, commercial enterprises, institutes, and magazines. It was success won by persistence, decisiveness, and endurance through long and difficult stretches of hard work. "When the work stops being fascinating and fun, and turns into an ordeal, then it is important to be professional and continue," she said. Enjoyment is the reward when the work and struggle are done.

Most of the younger female entrepreneurs want to realize their creative ideas and are usually more prepared to take risks than older women. Women generally start small to reduce risks, so many are just one-woman shows.

Short on cash, long on ideas Financing is one of the main problems. Banks sometimes find that the investment volume is too low or that there is no collateral to back up a loan.

Gisela Berger is a typical example. She quit her job as chief purchaser of a chain of stores when her daughter was born. Fifteen years later, she was 53 and widowed, and had difficulty getting a job. Short on savings, she finally decided to start a second-hand clothes store. She bought clothes by weight for just a few Deutschmarks from the Red Cross and refurbished them. (Germans often give away clothes in excellent condition to charities.) It provided her with a comfortable pension and paid for her daughter's medical schooling.

Networking in business Women have to deal with a lot of prejudice at work. Networks give businesswomen and managers not just moral and practical support through training, information, work groups, and contacts, but also boost their image through better publicity. Networking is spreading to many towns in Germany.

Law

Women have been laying down the law in Germany since 1922, when Maria Munk became the first female assistant judge. Anita Augsburg, who came before her, as the first German female lawyer and vice-president of the General German Women's Association, had to take her degree in Switzerland since women were not admitted to German colleges till 1901.

Untainted women After World War II, women jurists worked as defense counsels in military courts in West Germany. Since they were not allowed to work in the judiciary during the Nazi regime, they were politically untainted and could take over posts as judges in municipal, district and appeal courts after the war. Women jurists also found their way into various federal courts and political parties.

Now, almost 50 years later, women in legal robes are a common sight. One out of every five state attorneys and judges is a woman. (Women in the east had the advantage—before unification of the two Germanies, about 50% of the judges in East Germany were women.) There are still few female judges in the federal courts, but if we take into account the increasing numbers of female students making a beeline for law studies in the last decade, young female jurists are making their way up.

Vacancy: women only

Law is one field where old taboos have fallen, though some stubble remains. Gisela Niemeyer (right), a judge in the Federal Constitution Court from 1977 to 1989, married while studying and had a son and a daughter in between exams. Her husband, also a law student then, helped with the children. It was unusual at the time, and when he was out with the pram, he was often pitied: "So young and already a widower," people murmured.

After graduating, she had trouble getting a job. "Can you imagine a woman as a financial director?" she was asked at one interview. Her break came through the women's emancipation movement of the 1970s. Then, being a highly qualified woman was the precondition for three of her jobs. She became the first female judge in the Federal Income Tax Appeal Tribunal in Munich in 1972. In 1975,

she was asked to be the president of the Fiscal (Tax) Court in Duesseldorf. In 1977, she took over the vacant post of the previous female judge at the Federal Court of Constitution.

As late as 1984, Maria Peschel-Gutzeit had to fight to be the presiding judge at the Appellate Court in the Second Senate of Hamburg when a concerted action by its male members tried to bar her candidacy in 1984. She learned to be strong at this time. "Women must learn to enter a conflict … and not always take rejections personally. And they have to realize it's not enough just to do their work well," she said. She is used to getting what she wants. At 57, she obtained a doctorate at the University of Freiburg and is now the only woman among 90 authors of a civil rights commentary. She has also had to juggle her career with three children, because, she says, "There was no part-time job for judges then." She and her first husband, also a judge, made a perfect relay team, exchanging their son at a gas station in Hamburg between pre-arranged work and family shifts. The justice senator since 1991 and ex-president of the German Women Jurists' Association intends to increase the proportion of women in the ranks of judges.

Iron nerves

Being constantly in the middle of conflicts gives women jurists iron nerves and courage. Unlike most of her female colleagues, who are in civil and family courts, Johanna Dierks is one of the few women in jury court. She has been the presiding judge of the Court of Assizes for more than 15 years and is responsible for homicide cases. Johanna Dierks has had a heavy book hurled at her head by a man she sentenced, and has been threatened by others. Yet she says, "I am afraid of thunder, but not of the accused. They belong to my job." For rape victims, particularly, this judge is a sensitive and understanding woman first. It is not often that sensitive women's issues are handled by women judges, however, as there are still too few of them in Germany.

Many female lawyers and judges are leading politicians in parliament, five federal states have female justice ministers, and, since May 1992, there is a female federal minister of justice.

Judicial influence Through their presence in judicial and political fields, women are able to shape legislation and improve the fate of other women. Most of them are organized into the strong German Women Jurists' Association. They are one jump ahead of the state in issues important to women. Being in the arena daily, they see the wrongs and try to right them by drafting and presenting the laws even before society is ready to recognize the need for them.

Medicine

In the cold efficiency of ultra-modern hospitals, tender care and concern are medicines that help patients recover faster.

Medicine is a profession calling for many years of training and long hours of work and commitment. This makes it difficult for women to balance family and a medical career. Yet there has been a dramatic surge in the number of female doctors in the past few years, overtaking the incremental rate of male doctors. Today, about half the new medical students are female, as are about a third of hospital doctors and a quarter of those in practice. In the New Federal States, the proportion is even higher, and this may broaden the thin ranks of leading women doctors and medical professors in time to come.

Women doctors are expected to specialize in fields calling for sensitivity, like pediatrics, psychology and anesthetics. Research, surgery, and orthopedics (bone medicine) are done mainly by male doctors. Unlike in Russia, where it was deemed indecent for women to see male doctors for gynecological problems, in Germany, the majority of gynecologists are males.

Professor Dr. Ingeborg Falck is one of the rare few who have made it as a female chief executive of a hospital. In her first job at the Charité Hospital in East Germany, in 1945, she was put in charge of a clinic where "patients had to be treated on straw beds in windowless rooms." When the wall went up through Berlin, she headed west.

Within 18 months, she became chief physician for internal medicine at the Max Buerger Hospital. In 1981, she took charge of the 900-bed hospital in Berlin-Charlottenburg where most of her patients were the post-war "Rubble Women." Seeing how little had been done in the field of old-age problems, she then specialized in gerontology. Now retired, she remains active, publishing the *Journal of Gerontology* as well as doing advisory work on several commissions.

Medicine and politics For working mothers, part-time jobs are scarce, as hospitals do not have a budget for part-time doctors. Besides, hiring part-time doctors involves more administrative work.

Leading female doctors point out that this is mainly a matter of attitude. The benefit, for example, of having a fresh, efficient, and dedicated female surgeon work once or twice weekly, instead of over-exhausted doctors in attendance round the clock, is obvious.

As in many other fields, women in medicine still have to fight for more rights and against old prejudices. A small but strong body of highly energetic women has emerged: the Association of German Women Doctors. Its president since 1989, gynecologist and psycho-therapist Dr. Ingeborg Retzlaff, is also the only female president of a state medical chamber, a position she has held since 1981. Her chamber work includes lobbying and advanced medical training for doctors.

Dr. Ingeborg Retzlaff's love for political work began early. In 1951, she was the first woman to be elected president of a student association in a German college.

A cut above the rest

Up to 20 years ago, surgery was done by men only, but today electrical drills, saws, and lasers call for feeling and sensitivity rather than muscle power. While female surgeons are still a minority, their interest in surgery is growing. As far as stamina and decisiveness go, surgeons have to be a cut above the rest. As Dr. Ingrid Hasselblatt-Diedrich (right), chief surgeon in Frankfurt's Sachsenhausen Hospital, says, "To be a surgeon, one has to have a passion. ... Even though the path of a woman surgeon is still thornier than in other fields, it's a challenge, burden, and fulfillment at the same time."

Under such dedicated women, the Association of German Women Doctors has argued on many issues, including part-time work for mothers and refresher training so they can return to medicine after a "family pause." The Association does publicity and lobby work, and its annual conferences cover wide-ranging subjects such as "Women between Aggression and Depression" and "Women in the Modern World of Work."

"I am waiting for my soul to follow" Triple and quadruple responsibilities take their toll, however. Dr. Hedda Heuser-Schreiber, who does post-operative cancer therapy, was the president of the Association for 16 years till 1989 and also a member of parliament for seven years. She serves on a European Community commission and several federal commissions, and does journalistic and association work as well.

Her son says with pride, "My mother can do five things in one go." She herself tells the story of an Indian who rode in a car for the first time in his life, in New York. When his friend had parked the car, the Indian got out and lay down on the ground. Asked why, he answered, "I am waiting for my soul to follow." Hedda Heuser-Schreiber feels the same way about her hectic pace.

Politics

For years, female politicians in Germany have struggled within their parties for a greater share of power, with painfully slow progress. Then came the ecological Green party, co-founded by the charismatic Petra Kelley, that teemed with women from the feminist movement. In the 1980s, they twice organized an all-female committee to represent the party in parliament. One of these was led by ex-pastor and agricultural expert Antje Vollmer, who said they wanted to try out a new style of politics, with cooperation rather than competition and personality cults.

Through their strong showing in the 1987 election, the number of women in parliament rose to more than 15% for the first time since 1919. Greater improvement is likely now that quotas are slowly becoming accepted as an effective way of clearing a path for

Petra Kelley, co-founder of the Green party.

Female politicians do not focus only on women's issues. Their power and influence come from being experts in many fields. Ingrid Matthaeus-Maier (left), a judge, is a highly respected finance and nuclear expert. Anke Fuchs is an expert in labor law, and social and pension politics. Hertha Gmelin-Daeubler is a specialist on legal rights and many other issues. Hildegard Hamm Bruecher is an expert on education systems.

women in all walks of life. Of the prominent political parties, the Social Democratic Party plans to reserve 40% of party functions for women by 1994, and the Green women already have a 50% quota. The Christian Democratic Union and the Free Democratic Party are against quotas, but plan to share functions in proportion to female membership in the party.

Women in parliament Since 1961, starting with Dr. Elisabeth Schwarz-haupt as the minister of health, there

Rita Suessmuth with federal chancellor Helmut Kohl. *Suess* is German for "sweet," and the press has nicknamed her "Sweet Rita."

have always been women in the cabinet and as state secretaries. Anne Marie Renger became the first president of the parliament in 1965. No woman has as yet headed a political party at the national level, but the next election may bring this about. The very popular

Renate Schmidt is already chairman of the Social Democratic Party in ultra-conservative Bavaria.

Women: a political issue Through internal pressures and the international focus on women started by the United Nations declaration of 1975 as the International Year of Women, women have become a political issue. One result is that, in every state and most institutions, organizations and unions, there are "equal opportunity" offices to ensure better chances for women. Now almost every state has a "minister for women."

Women politicians have traditionally been put in charge of the welfare of women, health, and family. But recently, defense, foreign affairs, housing, as well as the chancellery, have seen women in responsible positions. In 1989, in Berlin, the city of happenings and change, women senators were in the majority—a political milestone for women.

"Sweet Rita" While many women worked their way up through years of loyal party work, some have jumped from outside jobs into politics. Rita Suessmuth (born 1937), was a professor in educational science issues when she was hired by the ruling Christian Democratic Union party as an expert on family affairs. She became the federal minister for youth, family, women and health, and in 1988, president of the parliament. She has been very feminist in her views and has put her weight behind reforms for women in spite of strongly traditional party thinking.

Modern "Rubble Women" In the New Federal States, where unity has brought great political, economic, and social changes, newcomers like the physicist and minister for women, Angela Merkel, have risen to meteoric heights in a short time. Another is the Social Democratic Party's Regine Hildebrandt, a biologist and a woman with no pretensions, who goes straight to the heart of the matter. People in the streets say, "She is the only one who has done something for us." The usually sympathetic minister for work and social affairs has no patience with whiners. "Good heavens! One has to do something and not just sit and wait around for things to happen," she says.

Regine Hildebrandt, a politician who believes people should help themselves.

In the eastern sector, women were the first to be let go when jobs were slashed. Luckier ones are burdened with balancing work and children as child-care centers have closed down through lack of funds. There, the political cry is:
"Women who don't take action,
Must work in the kitchen."

Trade unions

Trade unions in Germany fight for greater equality for women in the work place, but, ironically, women have been under-represented in union posts. Demands for a quota ruling have become louder, with some positive results. The Association of German Employees, for example, plans to reserve 40% of union posts at all levels for women and 40% for men—then it's a free-for-all for the remaining 20%.

One of the earliest women trade unionists, Emma Ihrer (1857–1911), was just 24 when she started being active in union work. To organize self-help for women, she founded an association to represent the interests of women workers. She also began the journal, *The Female Worker*.

Confusing goals German unions represent people in various professions in an age when attitudes and technology are changing rapidly. Consequently, those defining union goals have many pitfalls to avoid.

When unions tried to protect women by restricting or banning some types of work, feminists said the bans fenced women in and stopped them from gaining equality. Many employers agree, especially since too many protective regulations increase the cost of hiring women. While feminists say adult women must be allowed to make their own decisions, others fear women will be pressured to accept work that may affect their health.

Women's gripes Unionists have had their work cut out for them in Germany. After the law for equality took effect, the classifying of wages into "skilled workers, unskilled workers, and women" was removed in 1955, but came in through the back door as "light wage groups." Since 1988, this particular category has been disallowed. Yet women workers are still often in the lowest pay category, and unionists must scrutinize wage bargaining clauses to ensure women are placed in the right grouping. They also try to push through programs like upgrading and part-time work. Through changes in the industry, few women now do the same work as men, so the unions have changed their motto and are asking for "equal pay for *equivalent* work" for women.

Unions have been trying to help women balance family and work, cope with unemployment, and fight for better working conditions, better pay, and more job opportunities and training. They have been able to extend child-upbringing leave from 18 months to 2–7 years in many of the larger business groups. Recent increases in union numbers reflect new women members. Clearly, women are seeing the positive gains of organized lobbies.

Monika Wulf-Mathies

The first woman union chief, the president of the OeTV, the public service and transport union, has headed one of Germany's biggest trade unions, representing nurses, garbage collectors, civil servants, bus drivers, skilled workers, and others, since 1982. Monika Wulf-Mathies' appointment also marked the first time that an OeTV leader was not chosen from the rank and file of workers but from an academically educated younger generation. In tough negotiations, her bargaining skills and integrity are highly respected. She has been re-elected three times with clear majorities and is one of Germany's most powerful leaders.

Monika Wulf-Mathies first worked for the nation's leaders, writing speeches on economic and social policies, and became an active union member. In 1976, she managed social and health policies and women's interests in the union, and started a campaign to counter the discrimination against women in the civil service. "The reason why women find it hard to get to the very top is not through lack of ability or education, but because of the prejudices and discrimination against them," she declared.

She should know. She herself has often been confronted with sexist remarks and questions like, "What does your husband think of your holding such a high post?" She would snap, "Well, would you ask a man in a similar position what his wife would think?" What she calls "textile-journalism" annoys her. Seeing descriptions of her fingernails, her stockings, and her clothes, she once asked, "And who writes about the socks of the chancellor?"

Today, the task of the OeTV is huge. With the unification of the two Germanies, it now has to look after 420 different types of professional groups and 2.3 million members, and it is becoming more difficult to represent the interests of all the members properly. But despite the extremely heavy work load and the stress, the perfectionist remains undaunted.

Missionary welfare

A nun with a deep compassion for prostitutes and the down-and-out, Dr. Lea Ackermann first became aware of the problem in the Philippines, where daughters were sold off by poor farmers. She watched Filipino nuns talk to girls at bus-stops and on the street, offering them job training and education as a start to a new life. Back in Germany, she started a forum on the problems of these girls.

Later, in Mombasa, Kenya, Lea Ackermann built a women's center out of a run-down warehouse. It gave prostitutes there an alternative way of earning a living by sewing, pottery, and making bread or ice-cream. "I want to give them a new self-respect," she said. Other centers sprang up in Rwanda, Nairobi, and Ghana.

Back in Germany again, she initiated SOLWODI in 1987: Solidarity with Women in Distress, a network for prostitutes of third world countries, and a center for Asian and African girls. The project includes many Thai and Filipino women who are forced into brothels after being lured to Germany with promises of marriage. Lea Ackermann lobbied actively against "sex tourism" and advertisements for such marriages.

Above: Dr. Lea Ackermann relaxing at one of her centers in Africa.

Welfare

"You can't imagine what a little hand-holding and a caress does for them," says housewife volunteer Lena Wiegert after a visit to an old people's home. Another woman volunteer helps a young housewife do her housework and takes her three small children out for a walk once a week, while "Women in Green" visit patients in hospitals.

Each year, more than half a million tired mothers are able to take a holiday at the "Muttergenesungswerk" (MOO-ter-geh-NAY-soongs-verk), a foundation for the recuperation of mothers, thanks to Elly Heuss-Knapp (1881–1951), nicknamed "the Mother of Mothers." She started the foundation in 1950 to give mothers a chance to rest and recover their strength and spirit in peaceful surroundings.

Volunteers There where cheerful help is needed, women put out a helping hand. The volunteer service of women in social welfare work is not only invaluable in psychological and social terms, but it also saves the state an estimated 14 billion dollars a year. Women make up 60% of the estimated 2 million volunteers in church, welfare groups, neighborhood help, and other organizations. As the cost of social welfare goes up, women are being called to do more voluntary social work.

Many of them are between 40 and 60 and contribute from 20 to 45 hours a month. Employed women are more likely to be on committees, and housewives do more of the hands-on work. Apart from the help they give, many of these women find this work represents a meaningful activity.

Professionals About a hundred years ago, Minna Cauer and Jeanette Schwerin began to train women for the administration of welfare work, and in 1908, Alice Salomon started the first school for social work for women. Since then, welfare work has become a profession for women as well. Now two-thirds of professional social workers are women. As part of the general policy of giving women better opportunities, most welfare organizations have been trying to introduce the 50% quota in hiring and management policies since the 1980s.

Welfare projects include work with youths, prisoners, foreigners, old people, and children, as well as drug and alcohol therapy and therapy for battered women.

Helping women prisoners has been a central focus of Professor Dr. Helga Einsele, who headed the women's prison in Frankfurt from 1947 to 1975. She and her colleagues worked to give women prisoners liberal and humane treatment. Training and education were provided, and children under 6 were allowed to live with their mothers. This policy has been continued as "open prisons." Even after her retirement, Dr. Einsele worked in projects for released women prisoners and for the reform of prisons. For her, social and psychological support—"not punishment but help"—is a convincing alternative.

Dr. Helga Einsele in her garden.

Emma with its publisher, Alice Schwarzer. The magazine stays clear of traditional women's topics such as gardening, and carries stories of women in unusual lines of work.

Media

The opinion makers are still men, but criticism in the 1970s about the lopsided presentation of women in the media has caused positive changes on and off television, radio, and newspapers.

On television, more women are reading and editing the news, hosting talk shows, presenting quizzes and events as showmasters, or discussing political, economic, and social questions. On the other hand, soap operas with women in traditional roles have a large following among female viewers.

Studies show that women have had more exposure as show presenters on commercial than on public television. The former present their news as entertaining "news shows," and attractive, fashionable women with a personal approach contribute to this image. In shows where seriousness and objectivity are to be conveyed, men in conservative clothes are used. Women in the media are associated more with leisure, daily life, and art than sports and adventure. They are still under-represented in shows on politics and economics.

Radio broadcasts now give more time to women's issues, but the press appears to be sticking to its old success formulas of beauty and cosmetics, recipes, gardening, and "tear-duct" romances. A number of political and business magazines now feature women leaders on a regular basis, while feminist magazines like *Emma* and *Ypsilon* prefer controversial themes and keep the emancipation issue alive.

Single life for women journalists About 50% of new trainees are women. Career opportunities for female journalists are far better than before at the middle management and editorial levels, but not in top management. Most women quit high pressure jobs at about 30 to start a family or become freelance journalists, dropping out of the running at an age when the climb up the management ladder really starts to get steep. Like those in business management, women journalists have less of a family life than their male counterparts, most of whom are married and have children. The (Women) Equality Offices are exploring ways of helping women, for example, though finding part-time jobs for women even at higher levels, and calling for company-run kindergartens.

Two media profiles

Lea Rosh One woman who has reached the top in the media world is journalist and ex-talkmaster Lea Rosh (right). She was appointed director of the broadcasting station, Norddeutscher Rundfunk, in Hanover, in February 1992. She has a reputation for defending minorities like gypsies, homosexuals, and Jews, and for creating a stir in other red-hot issues. Her recent appointment as director calls for a change of focus to administrative work and is another political signal for German women.

Marion Doenhoff Nicknamed the Red Countess, this aristocratic journalist and publisher born in 1909 has become a semi-monument. After a spectacular horseback escape from Russian troops to West Germany, she joined the newly founded newspaper, *Die Zeit*, as a journalist.

The countess went on to head the influential political desk, and later became the paper's managing editor, then publisher. "As a journalist," she said, "I can achieve more than a member of parliament ... [who] ... has only one vote." She believes in keeping the government under perpetual scrutiny, and her political comments command great respect. One journalist paid her the tribute of knowing "how to say great and important things simply and with an undertone of humor." Historian Golo Mann said simply, "She is one who does not open up old wounds, but builds bridges and searches for solutions."

Literature

At the same time as it reveals the secrets of the writers, literature shows the social changes of their time. In the Middle Ages, most of the writings of women in Germany concerned religion as it dominated their lives. Besides, it was one of the few forms of writing allowed them. In the 17th century, women like Sybilla Schwarz wrote poems for special occasions. Since domestic duties were women's responsibilities, female poets or their male relatives had to declare in the preface that no housework had been neglected as the poetry was composed either during their youth or while doing housework.

The popularity of novels in the 19th century opened new avenues for women writers. Later writings of German women dealt with social problems and emancipation.

Post-World War II literature has seen an outbreak in many directions. The harrowing war experience was the theme of many books, especially those of Jewish writers like Nelly Sachs (see opposite) and Anna Seghers (born 1900), who became a staunch socialist in East Germany. In East Germany, women writers focused on the lives of women in socialism and the conflicts that came from the splitting of Germany into East and West.

Traditional and feminist literature

Until recently, women were portrayed in domestic roles, as obedient, hardworking and loving wives or mothers.

A sharp break with this tradition came during the women's movement of the 1970s. Women grew aware of their inferior position and searched for literature expressing female suffering and subjugation as well as their new experiences, but well-known writers of the time did not offer them comfort. They still spoke of old roles and conflicts, insecurity, and pain within the traditional values.

Then new writers emerged as well as a new style of writing. The use of "I," not "we," and subjectivity were emphasized. A typical example of documentary writing is Schwarzer's *Der kleine Unterschied und seine grossen Folgen* (*The Little Difference and its Great Consequences*), in which women of different social classes relate their experiences in their traditional feminine roles.

Haeutungen (*Moulting*) by another writer, Verena Stefan, was identified

Annette von Droste-Huelshoff's (1797–1848) writings are classic school literature today. Her deeply poignant poems show her love and keen observation of nature and give a glimpse of her own romantic, lonely heart. One of her most famous books is *Die Judenbuche* (*The Jewess Birch*).

Mastering the Nazi trauma

Nelly Sachs (1891–1970), Germany's first woman Nobel Prize winner for literature, was a Jewish writer who almost did not escape from the Nazis in 1940. Her transit visa for Sweden and the order for her transport to a concentration camp arrived at the same time. When she and her mother reported to the Gestapo (German secret police), the officer in charge advised them to fly out immediately and not take the train as it might be stopped at the border. They caught the last plane out of Berlin to Stockholm. There she made a living as a writer and translator of Swedish lyrics.

Already 50, she started a new phase of intense creativity. She had had news of friends, neighbors, and her secret lover—all perished in gas chambers. Turning away from her romantic lyrics of younger days, she wrote instead of the horrors done to Jews. "Writing was my mute outcry," she said. In one of her most famous poems ("O the Chimneys"), she wrote about the burning of Jews in concentration camps, "When Israel's body drifted as smoke/Through the air." When her pain had been mastered, she wrote of reconciliation. Her new works were described by Chancellor Heinrich Luebke as "works of forgiveness, of deliverance, of peace" in 1965, when Nelly Sachs became the first woman to be awarded the Peace Prize of the Booksellers' Association.

In 1960, she returned to Germany for the first time since her narrow escape, to Dortmund to receive the Annette von Droste-Huelshoff Prize for Poetry. Later, the city started a Nelly Sachs Award for Literature and paid her a pension. In 1966, at 75, she was awarded the Nobel Prize for Literature together with Israeli writer Shmuel Yosef Agnon. She died on May 12, 1970, still haunted by the holocaust.

with the women's movement. "I trotted everywhere with him to be near him, to all meeting places and pubs of the leftist ghettos ... With me he slept. Speaking, thinking, discussing, researching—that happened with others," said the heroine in *Haeutungen*.

Through its success, the book helped open up the market for feminist literature.

Right: Author Christa Wolf, whose books were criticized for being either against or for the socialist regime. Despite criticism, they are very popular throughout Germany.

In the later 1970s, traditional writers enjoyed renewed popularity. Now modified tradition and feminism sell side by side, and women writers almost dominate the book market.

Socialist literature: a dialogue On the other side of the wall, in East Germany, authors wrote about the experiences of women in socialist Germany. Although officially women were said to be emancipated, many contradictions deeply affected them. In Maxie Wander's *Guten Morgen Du Schoene* (*Good Morning You Beautiful*), apparently successful women revealed doubts and fears behind their facade of the perfect socialist woman. A young writer, Rita Kuczynski, in *Wenn ich kein Vogel waer'* (*If I Weren't A Bird*), talked of her experiences in a divided

Germany after the war. At the same time, these women believed in the socialist system. "… a woman with character can only be a socialist," declared writer Irmtraud Morgner. Authors, like artists and musicians, were promoted by the state, but their work was censored. They might be attacked for not adopting the government line, or their books banned for being too critical of the system. Like poet Sarah Kirsch, they could fall from grace and lose all means of earning a living and be forced into exile.

Christa Wolf (born 1929) was one of the most popular writers in both Germanies. One of her most well known books, *Der geteilte Himmel* (*The Divided Heaven*), discussed social and political problems in a love story. *Nachdenken über Christa T* (*Quest for Christa T*) was interpreted as anti-East German, and the book was criticized in her country. After unification, when her book *Was bleibt* (*What remains*) appeared, the unfortunate writer was attacked by West German critics for publishing an autobiographical book on police harassment only after it was all over. One of Germany's most famous writers, Günther Grass, says her criticism of the socialist regime was not as strong as others', but her style of careful persuasion was effective. Because she was read by Germans from east and west, she created a dialogue through literature. Her books are still widely read today.

Music and dance

Fine music—religious music, for example—used to be the monopoly of the church and the state and thus closed not only to women but common people. (The latter were only allowed folk music.) Female parts were sung by eunuchs. But when Italian opera became popular in the 17th century, the lilt of female voices thrilled audiences in a way even the best eunuchs' voices could not.

After the French Revolution and the crumbling of feudalism, music was open to the masses. In the 18th century, the popularity of French culture grew, and piano playing by women in the privacy of the home became fashionable.

While women's music performance was applauded, only men were believed capable of good music composition, an attitude still affecting Germany's music world. Compositions by women were labelled "lyrically sentimental." Until recently, it was difficult to find the works of even three of the most productive of 19th century women composers: Fanny Hensel, Josephine Lange, and Johanna Kinkel. Female German musicians now hold festivals regularly to promote their work and have set up their own music archives.

East German artists were luckier. They could compose for five years at state expense, and there were special promotional programs for young composers that gave both men and women equal exposure. The state also organized concerts and media publicity.

One of the most famous and outstanding composers there is Ruth Zechlin (born 1926), who has composed more than 200 works for orchestra, chamber ensemble, opera, piano, organ, and cembalo (harpsichord), among others. Her analytical style has been partly a result of the strict Bach School she attended in Leipzig, and partly her immense musical knowledge. Ruth

Composer Ruth Zechlin running through a piece with some musicians.

Anne-Sophie Mutter, in her most famous pose.

Zechlin maintains a controlled balance between emotions and the intellect. She says, "There is no question of man or woman when I judge music, only that of quality of the work of art."

Anne-Sophie Mutter A German musician who has achieved world fame is Anne-Sophie Mutter (born 1963). She had her first violin lesson at 6, won a prize in a federal contest at 7, and began her international career at 13. When she was 18, the first Anne-Sophie Mutter Society was founded in Japan. At 22, she was made an honorary member of the Royal Academy of Music in London. She is first at the Academy to hold the International Chair of Violin Studies.

Anne-Sophie Mutter has been compared to the violin genius Yehudi Menuhin, and critics rave over her effortless "singing legato." In her quest for perfection, she is self-critical without allowing herself to be neurotic. When she is on stage, the work process is done and the total artist takes over.

Nimble feet Free dance, like many of the other arts, was destroyed by the Nazis, but new studios came up slowly again. The Dance Forum in Cologne, the Mary Wigmann Studio, and the Folkwang School in Essen were the most prominent. The student revolt of the late 1960s brought feminist expression into choreography that did

Musical gender

Music principles and terms were divided into the active, extrovert masculine, and the still, introvert feminine. "Female" passages included lyrical melodies, legatos, and those using harps and flutes. Chamber music, filigree-like instruments, and even rhythms are "female." "Male" passages have large interval leaps, upward striving notes, louder tones, octaves, and they involve the use of wind and brass instruments.

Orchestras used to be a never-never land for women, except for harpists. Some conductors still claim women do not have the lung power for the larger wind instruments, and brass instruments are still dominated by men. Now there are many women musicians in all divisions.

away with role division of the sexes in classical ballet, and women headed new dance schools.

Gret Palucca The Palucca school is one such school. Gret Palucca (born 1902), teacher and choreographer, was one of the first students of the expressionist dancer, Mary Wigmann, in Dresden. It was said of Palucca that "No German dancer has her body so much in control ... owns such changes of expressions from the tenderest, dreamy devotion to the highest steely jump." The Palucca school in Dresden was bombed in 1945, but Gret Palucca started a new school immediately after the bombing. It has taught the greatest number of dancers in East Germany.

Pina Bausch One of the leading talents of the dance scene in Germany today is Pina Bausch. A dancer with great intensity and expression, Pina Bausch's poetry is in her eyes and body in dance. Born in Solingen in 1940, she studied dancing from the age of 15 under Kurt Jooss, and in America in the Juillard School of Music. In 1962, she returned to Germany to join the newly founded Folkwang Ballet and began choreographing in 1968. Since 1973, she has been the director of the Tanztheater Wuppertal Pina Bausch.

Using irony and humor, Bausch's themes deal with the conflict between the sexes and classes. Her dance requires no movement, but may be simply a way of holding the body. At first, her interpretation of dance was so unusual, the audience booed, but now her Tanztheater in Wuppertal has become a place of pilgrimage and "la Bausch" is a near legendary figure in international dance.

Pina Bausch, whose interpretation of dance startled audiences.

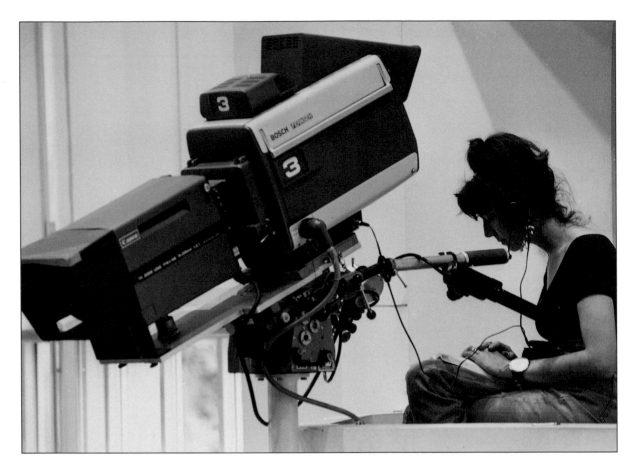

A camerawoman checks her script. Women bring both technical and creative skills to movie production.

Movie production

Making movies is almost unthinkable without women. Scores of them are busy on and off sets as scriptwriters, cutters, camerawomen, and movie directors. In recent years, female students in movie academies outnumbered men, but there are still very few women on boards deciding on movie subsidies.

During the women's emancipation movement of the 1970s, some of the newer generation, like Helke Sander, Dorris Doerrie, Helma Sanders-Brahms, and Jutta Brueckner, made feminist movies to create awareness. They felt there was a need to show women from a female point of view and to correct the stereotyped image of women in movies. In the beginning, documentary movies were made because women wanted more publicity for women's issues.

Margarethe von Trotta Among those who wrote their own scripts was Margarethe von Trotta. Born of a Russian aristocratic immigrant in 1942, she married Voelker Schloendorf, a well-known movie producer, and not only co-produced and co-wrote with him and another famous producer, Werner Fassbinder, but acted as well. She "emancipated" herself professionally by producing her own movies with female themes. Some of these are *The Second Awakening of Christa Klages*, *Sisters or the Balance of Luck*, *Leaden Times*, and *Rosa Luxemburg*. She has received many awards, including the Golden Lion prize in Venedig and the German Film Band in gold.

Dorris Doerrie One of the most important movie-makers in Germany, after Werner Fassbinder, is Dorris Doerrie. Born in 1955 in Hanover, she went to America to train in acting and studied theater and movies in California. Apart from documentaries, she has produced highly successful feature movies. Three movies, *Men*, *Paradise*, and *Happy Birthday Turk*, brought her international fame and offers from Hollywood. She refused them, preferring to go on making movies over which she had control. Dorris Doerrie is strictly individual and only makes movies where she can write or adapt the stories herself.

Leni Riefenstahl (born 1902) began her career as a dancer but switched to acting after a knee injury. In 1931, she took up filming and *The Blue Light* won her a gold medal in the 1932 Venice Biennale.

Her downfall came after she made brilliant movies for Hitler, like *Triumph of the Will*, about the 1934 Nazi rally at Nurenberg, and *Olympia*, about the 1936 Olympics in Berlin. After some years shadowed by her Nazi association, Leni Riefenstahl made a comeback with her work on the Nuba tribe, followed later by an underwater movie.

Award-winning movie producer Margarethe von Trotta.

Sports

If you don't take the edge with full aggression, says national skier Katja Seizinger, you will be "mincemeat." She flies a chilling 130 feet to catapult down an icy slope at 60 miles an hour. Women get back on their feet again after accidents that snap every ligament in the knee and break enough bones to cripple a person for life.

Not long ago, the idea of sports for women was met with clucking about grace, beauty, childbearing, and health. When all-woman soccer was started, clubs letting women play were banned

Drug abuse is a worldwide problem, as the 1992 Olympics in Barcelona showed. American sports doctor Randy Eichner testified in his speech, "Dying to win," how thousands of top athletes are prepared to die for victory. A macabre motto of champion cyclists, 18 of whom died of a new drug in Holland and Belgium, was "Better dead than second."

from the Soccer Association. Greater tolerance, more leisure time, health consciousness, and media coverage of stars like tennis ace Steffi Graf, ice skater Katarina Witt, and gold medalist high jumper Heike Henkel have changed this attitude, with the result that today there is almost no division between male and female sports. Although training and competitions of sports clubs and associations have men's and women's divisions, in schools and colleges sports has become mostly co-educational. In East Germany, women athletes underwent the same training programs as the men.

German women are more active in gymnastics, riding, swimming, volley-ball, light athletics, tennis, and skiing. Women are still under-represented in management and committees. They become less active in high performance sports as they grow older because of family priorities, lack of time, or for physical reasons.

In the media, women's sports are still attracting less attention—only about 7%—than men's sports.

Drug abuse German sports has been rocked in the past by drug abuse scandals. Officials, doctors, and athletes obsessed with victory believed winning came not just from training, but also from male hormones and anabolic steroid drugs. Promising girls put by trainers and doctors on the anabolic list from as early as 16 years swayed between death and manliness for years. Replying to comments on hunky women swimmers at the Montreal Olympics in 1976, the East German trainer said, "They're not here to sing."

Learning to win clean is a slow process, but with greater public scrutiny, changes are in store.

Professional sportswomen

Steffi Graf Born in 1969, Steffi Graf has dominated international tennis for many years and her much feared serves have reached 100 miles an hour. At 4 or 5, she started hitting balls above the two armchairs her father pushed against a basement wall. When she managed to get 20 balls over them in succession, she was rewarded with a party and raspberries on ice. She enjoyed this so much that when her father came home from work she would be waiting for him with her sawn-off tennis racket and a ball to get her 20 hits. At 13, she was already a world class player.

Anja Fichtel has brought in many medals for Germany. She started to train in fencing at 9. "I trained hard for 10 years and concentrated only on success, and saw nothing else," she said. It was a rigorous diet of fencing and smiling the whole time, but she was often in a panic, thinking of failure. The agony and work paid off. In 1988, she won two Olympic gold medals in Seoul and was world champion twice.

No (apron) strings attached German women are getting over hurdles not only in sports. Women who have reached the top have more company as more women join their ranks. Since education became equal and an economic boom opened new avenues, women have been able to discard their aprons.

Yet, as they strive to do as well as men, the burden of being a woman at work becomes apparent; they have to make hard family choices men do not even face. The very awareness of the "home" disadvantage has aroused the fighting spirit of women leaders and brought some changes. Differences will probably always exist, but as successful women become increasingly visible, new formulas and solutions are being found.

chapter four

Being Woman

n the earlier chapters, we saw something of the attitudes of both men and women toward the changing roles of German women. We have also seen how, through government quotas and their own relentless demands, women have made gains in many fields. Even in the countryside, there is a greater partnership between men and women. Through a well developed educational system and infrastructure and greater mobility, sharp differences between rural and urban women no longer exist.

As German women are wrestling with new values, so are smaller groups of women in Germany like the Turks, gypsies, and Italians. They have a greater adjustment to make than German women, for they are also caught between two ethnic cultures—their own and traditional German culture. Their dilemma is one of minorities everywhere: to adopt their host culture or to cling to their ethnic customs—or find a comfortable place in between.

The German resettlers

Many Germans still live as minorities in the countries of Eastern Europe. Those who are German by citizenship or nationality have a right to live in Germany. This includes people whose parents, grandparents, or spouses are German, or who are German by birth, language, upbringing, and culture. Some speak German, while others may not know the language or the culture because they were not allowed to practice them.

A German resettler (*opposite*) and a Turkish woman (right), both in headscarfs.

Decades behind the times In their headscarfs, many first generation immigrant women look like copies of German women of half a century ago. Passers-by may be startled to see old women in very old-fashioned clothes sitting on benches outside blocks of high-rise apartments, just as they might have done outside their houses in villages in Russia or Rumania.

Their family and neighborhood ties are very strong, and they usually have conservative moral values retained from pre-war German society, like family orientation, religiousness, diligence, cleanliness, obedience, and productivity. Their disorientation in a changed Germany, worsened by language problems, is often resolved only after a few generations.

Adapting to change Adapting to German culture is difficult for the first generation. Many get work not matching their qualifications, if they can find work at all.

Then there is the sudden consumerism to cope with. In the socialist countries of Eastern Europe, basic necessities are not easily obtained. In Germany, on the other hand, it is Christmas every day. Immigrant parents do not know how to react to children who once could not dream of owning stereos and fashionable clothes. Renate Sprott, a teacher and resettler, believes

Opposite: Language classes are essential, since even getting around on public transportation and filling in forms can create problems.

not all old values should be thrown overboard. "Even in Germany nothing is for free. But this country gives you more possibilities to shape your life than at home … if one works actively along."

In spite of the first agonies of change, these women are usually energetic and show great determination in helping the family settle in. After all, they have left a hard lifestyle behind them for a land that promises plenty.

Speechless Young immigrants also have to adjust. Some may have to repeat their education in German schools or go for further job training to fit into German work places. Many who did not speak German find themselves suddenly speechless. Young girls are often exposed early to the double burden on women, going to school in the mornings and looking after their younger siblings or doing housework in the afternoons. For girls, immigration has also meant greater parental control because they come from a more traditional and modest way of life. The most conservative are those from Russia, while those from Poland are more liberal.

Fortunately, these problems are temporary. Once the dust of change has settled and their lives have stabilized, the immigrants are usually happy they came. "When I am asked what nationality I have today, I am happy to say I am German," says one immigrant.

Russian Germans

The new wave of Russian Germans came to Germany only relatively recently. German colonies have existed in Russia since 1763, when Catherine the Great, a German princess and ruler of Russia, invited Germans over to the Volga to farm the land. In 1941, Stalin deported them from the blooming fields of the Ukraine and the Volga to desolate Siberia and to Kazakhstan where they suffered untold tortures. Even now, anti-German leaflets make their rounds, Germans are mugged, and cries of "Fascists!" are hurled at them. Hitler is not forgotten.

During celebrations, homemade German schnapps flows, old German songs are sung, and stories their grandmothers and grandfathers told are repeated. Their hearts are heavy with homesickness, but Germany is horror-struck at the thought of a mass influx of 2 million Russian Germans suddenly at its doorstep, all needing shelter and money to start a new life. To control the exodus, which is unique to the resettlers from Russia, Germany scrutinizes their ancestors and their habits in a 54-page form. "Baking an apple strudel is not proof of upkeeping the German tradition," one is told. The Russian Germans do not understand why Germany is slow to let them "go home." Those who finally arrive in Germany go through red tape, camps, cramped housing, and language courses, until a home and maybe a job are found.

The majority are strongly patriarchal farming people. Women traditionally marry young, have children, look after the household, and work as well. Girls are not given sex education, and parents and children are shocked by the liberal behavior of German youths. Russian German girls often do not get along with the local girls, and their parents forbid them to go to discos or out with German boys, whom they consider "fast."

Family unity and religious worship are strong. Many of the girls belong to an active and tightly knit Baptist community. They dress, talk, and act differently from the other Russian Germans, and they are not allowed to dance. As a result, they isolate themselves as a group. Social welfare groups try to help the girls adjust by working closely with their mothers as well, because parental control is powerful.

The Russian Germans are used to hardship and their patience seems endless. Now they can unpack their belongings sewn into bedsheets and tablecloths for they are finally "home." All they need to do is get used to it.

Interior of a gypsy caravan.

Minorities

Germany recognizes several minority groups like the Sorbs (a Slavic people who have lived in eastern Germany since A.D. 900, not to be confused with the Serbs), the Danish in Schleswig Holstein, and the Friesians. Their minority status is protected by law. They are well integrated with German society as they have lived with German neighbors for many centuries.

German gypsies

A less accepted German minority are the gypsies (Romanies and Sintis) who have been in Germany for more than 600 years. Contrary to popular belief, they are tax-paying German citizens and, like other citizens, they vote. But unlike the other minorities, they do not have political protection.

Language and religion Romanies and Sintis speak Romany, a language related to Sanskrit, as well as German, but their dialects are different so communication between gypsy groups may be difficult. They often adopt the religion of their host country. Some are Catholics, while most of those who came from Eastern Europe are Moslems.

Extended family Romanies and Sintis have close-knit, extended families whose members visit each other often. Long ago, the entire extended family—

Originally from northern India, gypsies have been a target of persecution almost everywhere. Hoping to escape inhumane treatment and extreme poverty in Eastern Europe, thousands of them have fled to Germany recently because of the country's liberal refugee laws and social benefits. Many Germans do not accept the refugee gypsies or their vagrant lifestyle. Because Germany's capacity to absorb refugees is at breaking point, its refugee laws are being revised and thousands of gypsies have been repatriated.

a patriarch with his children and their families—traveled together in caravans, but the post-war generation has settled down. Today, relatives live further apart. When they meet, music is a favorite pastime, and guitars, violins, and pianos are played and the old songs sung. The gypsies are very close to nature and greatly value family and children.

Gypsy woman   The gypsy woman is stereotyped by many people who imagine either a beggar in dirty rags or a beautiful, proud, and dangerous temptress.

Gypsy culture, in fact, has a strict tradition of purity for all actions. These range from the domestic (such as not washing bedding and dish towels together, one being for the body, the other for food) to the personal. Brides are expected to be virgins and their traditional sense of decency frowns on discussing matters of sexuality with men. For this reason, Sinti women (Sintezzas) who were force-sterilized by the Nazis could not be represented by Sinti men in their fight to be recognized as Nazi victims. The Sintezzas had to form a women's group to represent themselves.

Men of leisure   Historically, gypsy women were the ones who went out to work while the men stayed at home or played music at fairs, did wickerwork, restored violins, or traded in horses. The women earned money for daily expenses by begging, reading palms, selling herbs and handicrafts, or collecting scrap metal and other usable items. Working, they formed a bridge between the host society and their clan.

Homeless Romany woman and child on a sidewalk in Cologne.

Fatima Hartmann

As a sign of changing times, the chairperson of the Romanies and Sintis in Cologne is a woman. Fatima Hartmann, who married a German, has been living in Germany since 1968. "When we first moved here from Yugoslavia, my father forbade us to say we are Romanies." They feared the discrimination they had experienced in Yugoslavia. There the majority could not find jobs because they were gypsies and were forced to live in broken-down huts in slums, where their children played with toys made out of other people's discards. Since Fatima's father was a teacher, they lived in better conditions.

In Germany, other schoolchildren knew her as a Yugoslavian. Today, she stands up for her people. "It's time we fought for our culture and not let it disappear," says the social worker and freelance journalist whose first job was in a childcare center looking after children of many nationalities. "My dream is that grown-ups, too, can live so well together."

These days, their roles are reversed. The men are craftsmen or travel, selling antiques or restoring musical instruments. The women look after the home and children. In most families, married and usually elderly women guard the family fortune, represented long ago by the gold jewelry worn on their bodies.

Women were traditionally ranked lower than their fathers, husbands or brothers, and all decisions were made by an elderly male relative. A few of the younger, educated women are more independent; they expect their relationships with men to be more in the nature of a partnership.

Guest workers

Germany owes much of its economic well-being to the foreigners hired in the boom years of the 1950s and 1960s from Italy, Spain, Greece, Turkey, Portugal, and Yugoslavia. Most came alone and their families joined them years later. Today, three generations of these foreigners live in Germany.

"Home"—a generation question The pioneers had great problems adjusting, being disoriented by German culture and having to endure poor living conditions, overwork, and loneliness. Their inadequate qualifications landed them low-paying jobs.

They reacted by maintaining their ethnic lifestyle and rejecting German culture. "Going home" became central to all their efforts, and they worked hard to earn as much as quickly as possible. After staying in Germany for 10 or 20 years, some could still hardly speak German. They were consequently isolated and unable to learn new skills or take advantage of welfare programs. Since even reading bus signs required German literacy, some had trouble taking public transportation. Once home, though, they found to their chagrin that they had again become foreigners. They were seen as the *German* Greeks or *German* Italians, not Greeks or Italians. Many resigned themselves to going back only for vacations.

A lot has been done and continues to be done by social welfare and church groups to help foreigners fit into Germany. Those with problems can now ask for help in their own language.

Second-generation non-Germans fare better than the first. They know the language and act as translators for their parents, serving as buffers between their ethnic culture and the German one. Their dilemma is that they do not

Turkish women resting at the foot of a Beethoven memorial.

Turkish women shopping for food at a neighborhood market in Berlin.

know where they are finally going to live, and consequently they do not go for proper job training. Only half as many foreign girls as boys are in an apprenticeship program.

Third-generation non-Germans seldom have trouble fitting in. They are as well educated as Germans and are usually Western-oriented. Their German language is perfect, but their Greek or Turkish may be poor, and they have difficulty relating to their ethnic culture. For them, Germany is home.

A 20th century story Neval Yurtdas came from a little village in Anatolia, Turkey. She married young and had three children before she was widowed. Being practical, she taught herself to read and write and made sure her children studied hard at school.

When she heard how much she could earn in Germany, it seemed the answer to the problem of financing her children's education. She landed in Frankfurt, found a job as a cleaner, and learned German. A factory job followed, and soon the popular woman became a supervisor. Her children joined her in Frankfurt and enrolled in a German school. Now her daughter is studying medicine, a son is an engineer, and another son is studying computer science in a German college.

There are many immigrants like Neval Yurtdas: determined, courageous, and deeply committed to their children's success. But there are also many poor and uneducated immigrants who cling to old customs, growing more isolated as each succeeding generation changes its values.

Moslems in a Christian land

In Islam, women's honor is an important issue, one that makes a deep impact on how Moslem women conduct themselves. Men and women are segregated; a bride's virginity is a sign of her purity. In public, Moslem women must cover their bodies so that only the face is exposed to view. Their domain is in the home and men's outside; an exception occurs in rural areas where women help in the field. Today, however, education and modernization make it common for women to go out to work.

The Moslem Turks form the largest community of all foreigners living in Germany. In the 1960s and 1970s, thousands of Turkish women came to Germany alone as it was often easier for women to get a work permit than men. Their families joined them later. Having to cope alone has given many of these women independence and confidence. That and constant contact with the more liberal ways of the Germans have modified their attitudes and outlook.

Growing up German Many Turkish girls have grown up as Germans while their parents and grandparents have remained traditional Turks. The girls have to cope with two cultures, one shared with their German peers and the other with their Turkish family.

Teenaged Turkish girls are usually tightly controlled, not just by their parents but also by relatives, neighbors, and friends, most of whom came from the same village in Turkey and tend to live in the same German neighborhood. Going out or even being seen with boys is considered scandalous as girls are not allowed to be alone with a male not belonging to the same family. Marriage is often still prearranged by parents, and most marriages take place in Turkey with Turkish partners from home. Girls are usually married young.

The more religious and conservative girls accept this way of life, but some among them are attracted to the liberal ways of German girls seen daily in public, in schools, and on television. They question their traditions, and this leads to conflict at home because Islam demands that Moslem girls obey, without question, the head of their family, usually the eldest male. Today, many young Turkish girls in Germany not only wear jeans and fashionable clothes, but ask for more freedom. How these cultural clashes are resolved depends partly on the background and values of both the parents and their daughters.

Breaking out Parents from villages are likely to be deeply religious and strict. Their daughters are tradition-oriented, accept their role as homemakers, and conform to a traditional lifestyle. They mix with like-minded Turkish girls and hardly ever with Germans. Job training and education are irrelevant as they intend to marry and stay at home; sewing and cooking classes hold their interest.

Girls who attended only German school and had German playmates from an early age believe strongly in the German way of life. Some go through a crisis, having to choose between staying at home and suppressing their own wishes or breaking with their families. They usually have good job or educational qualifications because they see work as their passport to freedom. Many do eventually break completely with their families and marry Germans.

Germany is seeing an increasing number of parents, usually from larger towns in Turkey, who are liberally educated and not very strict. Their daughters grow up in a mixed lifestyle, somewhere between the Turkish and the German norms. They have friends in both groups. When cultural problems arise, these girls are usually prepared to thrash it out at home. While most Turkish parents tell their daughters they can only leave home with a bridal veil, a few have accepted that their daughters, like many German girls, want to move out and live with their boyfriends.

Dr. Saliha Scheinhardt

Born in 1950 in Konya, Turkey, to a devout Moslem family, Saliha had only one book at home—the Koran. Yet, at 15, she wrote her first short story, and at 17, she won the Youth Literature Prize of Konya. She came over to Germany with her German theology student husband, who had to convert to Islam to marry her. She worked in restaurants and factories, then studied educational science, and taught and did research on Turkish families.

In 1985, Saliha Scheinhardt won the Offenbach literature prize and became a resident writer for two years—the first foreigner in such a position in Germany. She has published six books in the German language, one of which has been made into a movie. Her books tell of the conflicts of Turkish women in Germany and in Turkey. Saliha Scheinhardt fights not just for oppressed women, but also for the oppressed miners of Anatolia.

The culture bridge The Germans themselves, especially the younger generation, are building bridges to their guest workers. Turkish-German, as well as other ethnic groups that include Germans, have sprung up all over Germany to counterbalance mindless racism.

However these girls resolve their conflicts and lead their lives, they are all, even those who live as Germans, fiercely proud of their Turkish origin.

Education The majority of the early guest workers came from poorer and mostly rural areas, had little education, and did not go through the German apprenticeship program. The younger Turks are better informed and educated.

Many official information brochures have been published in Turkish, and there are literacy and language courses to bridge the communication gap. Jobwise, girls tend to concentrate on tailoring or sales apprenticeships, although there is a trend toward jobs as doctors' assistants and in child care.

Nowadays, Turkish parents and children are more aware of the need for higher education. Increasing numbers of Turkish girls want to study in colleges, and their fathers appear to be more willing to permit this than before. In Germany, many Turkish women are doctors, translators, lawyers, business-women, shop owners, teachers, and writers who rank among Germany's most respected citizens.

Two young Turkish girls in Mosbach.

Yugoslavian women

The former Yugoslavians are the second largest group of foreigners in Germany. Since Yugoslavia was a multicultural and multinational country before it disintegrated in the early 1990s, there is no typical Yugoslavian woman.

Yugoslavians in traditional costume dance in a Berlin street. Ethnic clubs in German cities celebrate festivals in this way to foster cultural awareness among the people of their group.

Regional differences are strong; those from Slovania (formerly north Yugoslavia) have the outlook of industrialized Europeans, while many from Kossovo (formerly south Yugoslavia) are nearly as conservative as Turkish women from rural areas.

Attitudes to change Like Turkish women, many Yugoslavian women came to Germany alone, and the sacrifices and hardship they faced built their confidence. Although they live in a patriarchal society, this is colored by the socialist principles that give women equality. The divorce rate among German foreigners is highest for the Yugoslavians, and divorce proceedings are usually initiated by the women, who seem more dynamic and flexible than the men.

Many of the women are relatively well-educated, yet they often do not have better jobs, even after staying in Germany for 15–20 years. Although most of them speak and write German, their friends are mostly also from Yugoslavia.

Learning and integrating The parents have ambitions for their children and are well informed about education and job training vacancies for their daughters. The girls are equally ambitious. They know what career they want and work hard in school. Even girls who came over in their mid-teens learn the language fast.

Girls from northern Yugoslavia integrate quickly and try to adopt German habits, giving up their own ethnic ones. Their parents are usually tolerant of this attitude. The girls are sociable and prefer to go around with German girls of the same age. Southern Yugoslavians are more traditional in outlook and restrict their daughters' leisure activities and friendships with Germans. Girls from Yugoslavian Moslem families are often not allowed to mix with youths of other religions.

Mila Mrdovic is a hospital nurse. She came to Germany at the age of 10 when her father found a job in a car factory. After her mother had seen her children settled in school, she found herself a part-time job in a bakery. Mila and her brother learned German very quickly.

She soon got used to not wearing a school uniform and seeing children talk back to the teachers, which was unheard of in her Yugoslavian school. She enjoyed shopping, going to discos, or just visiting with German girls her own age. After school, she took up nursing, although her parents wanted her to be a doctor. Out of almost 200 applicants, only 45 were chosen, and Mila was one of them.

When she first came she did not understand German and felt like an outsider, but now Mila speaks the language like a German. In Germany, she misses the traditional warmth of Yugoslavians, but when she went to her grandparents' home on vacations in the past, she missed the comfort of Germany. When her Yugoslavian friends complain about Germany, she replies, "Why are you still here?" With Yugoslavia at civil war, Germany is home to more than Mila; her grandmother and other relatives are now in Germany too.

Italian women

German taste buds have been changed by the countless Italian restaurants, pizzerias, and ice-cream parlors run by Italian families, where mom or sometimes an aunt takes charge of the kitchen and papa and the children serve. Italian art, fashion, and artists add richness and variety to German cultural life.

Italians are almost on an equal footing with Germans in terms of social benefits. They do not need work and stay permits because Italy is part of the European Community, which allows citizens to move freely within the member states. Italians are mobile and their ties with Italy are very strong. This has given rise to a "pendulum phenomenon" as Italian guest workers move back and forth between Italy and Germany.

The majority of Italian workers who came to Germany in the 1950s and 1960s were from southern Italy. Many of them were poor and from a conservative rural background.

Traditional values The majority of Italian women in Germany work, but housework and children are also their responsibilities. Italians in Germany are very family-oriented.

Values in Italy have changed in the last few decades and women in Italy are now quite independent, but Italian workers who came to Germany from poorer and less educated backgrounds

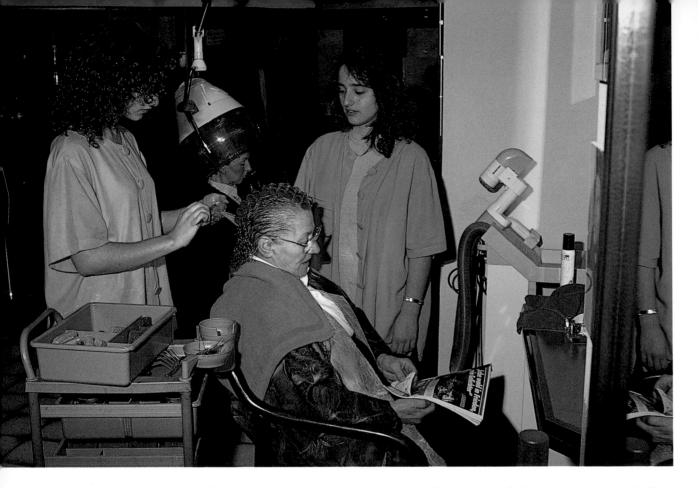

tend to retain the values they brought with them. Their daughters are often expected to marry young and start a family. Parents are strict with and protective of the girls, expecting them to spend their leisure time at home or with other Italian girls. They have great influence on the career choices of the girls, who attend German school in the morning and usually have Italian lessons in the afternoon. Italian girls who decide on vocational training opt for hairdressing, tailoring, or child care, and sometimes sales, but are discouraged from taking jobs that bring them into constant contact with male colleagues.

Recent trends In the past, many Italian parents did not understand the German school system, which is quite different from Italy's, and young Italians' education suffered from poor motivation. They now recognize the value of education in Germany and are more willing to accept changes.

With Europe coming closer together in economic and political cooperation, many highly educated, professional, and mobile Italian women have moved to Germany, attracted by better pay and business and work opportunities. This is likely to influence the Italian lifestyle in Germany even further.

Manuella Fideli is typical of the new generation of Italian women in Germany. Many Italian girls are among Germany's "popper" teenagers; this is an extremely fashionably dressed group. Manuella Fideli buys clothes for exclusive boutiques. This started when she returned from vacations in Italy with clothes that everyone went wild over. She speaks perfect German with an attractive Italian accent, and always looks as though she just stepped out of a fashion magazine. Her job takes her not just between two countries that Manuella considers home, but also to a greater "home" of international high fashion.

Greek women

Most of the older generation of Greek women came from the rural areas of northern Greece and have been in Germany for almost 30 years. Many have lost contact with Greece, but they have not put down roots in Germany either.

Greek values Tradition continues to guide Greek girls in Germany. Even second- or third-generation Greek parents in Germany tend to restrict their children in the manner of their own traditional upbringing.

In large German cities, Greek parents can often choose to send their children to Greek schools. Their aim is to have them pursue a higher education in Greece, and then work there. Partly because of different school schedules and partly because some parents fear the influence of liberal German attitudes, these children have little contact with German youths. Girls mix almost exclusively with other Greeks and attend festivals and activities organized by Greek associations.

In areas without a Greek school, the children attend German schools and, especially in rural areas, these children tend to go into job training rather than academic studies.

More and more, however, Greek youths want to make their own decisions, whether in their education or their lifestyle. Young Greeks are more willing and able to integrate than their parents, and each passing generation becomes more "Germanized."

Coming to terms

The minorities in Germany have had to come to terms with a rich, free, and modern yet uncompromisingly German Germany.

As the women among them learned to adjust to German values, they also had to meet the different expectations of their ethnic communities. For them, it is not merely a question of creating a niche for themselves in Germany, but also of tolerance if they wish to remain at the same time a part of their own community.

chapter five

Profiles of Women

The women featured in this chapter come from diverse fields and times, but all have chosen paths that required a strong conviction in what they were doing. For most of them, what they could achieve for others has been their goal. Often, they broke new ground in times when society was not ready to accept their efforts.

Most of them did not work alone. Their work represents the efforts of countless other women who either labored with them, or after them, paving new roads for Germans of a better age.

Ruth Pfau

In March 1960, it was 104°F and humidity was 80%. The chaotic Karachi airport and the cacophony of a bazaar did not help the airsick German nun. Dr. Ruth Pfau was sure she would not stay in Pakistan.

It took her three weeks to understand and be understood in English. Then a Mexican nun took Dr. Pfau to McLeod Road where the poorest of the poor vegetated—150 beggars with Hansen's disease, then called leprosy—in huts of cardboard, plastic bags, and bamboo sticks. The smells and the sights were nauseating: unfeeling, disfigured limbs on which rats gnawed at night; dirt, stench, vermin, fighting, and hashish. These were the patients of the Marie-Adelaide Leprosy Center (MALC) founded in 1953 by a French nun, Simone Fabry, and taken over by an American nun, M. Doyle, in 1958.

Opposite and right:
Ruth Pfau.

> **"The thought that hunger, homelessness, and poverty are not just a transition period but a constant condition from which there is no escape is horrifying."**
>
> —*Ruth Pfau*

Saving lives in a morgue Pieces of casing wood nailed together provided their dispensary and treatment room. There was no water or electricity, and two tiny windows did not quite remove the heat, noise, and stench of many bodies. It touched Dr. Pfau to see how even the patients who could only crawl through the dust accepted their fate.

Inside, the young doctor operated, beside her a patient whose task was to chase off flies with a bamboo swatter.

"I never thought I could do my work in such conditions just as well as in a modern hospital," she wrote.

Later, they moved their "operating theater" to cleaner quarters, the town hospital morgue. Medicine came from Germany, and eventually money was available to buy a small hospital in town. Expecting protests from neighbors, they sneaked in after dark with a few sticks of furniture. Once there, not even the neighbors' abuse and court cases could budge them.

Shared suffering Ruth Pfau was born in 1929, in Leipzig, the fourth child of six. She was 4 when the Nazis came to power, and 10 when war broke out. The schoolgirl joined the BDM, the Nazi-

Right and opposite: Ruth Pfau works in unusual conditions, seeing patients in open spaces and remote mountain settlements.

run Federation of German Girls. Ruth's ideal was their group leader, until, one day, her group discussed Nietzsche and adopted a statement from his writing: "The greatest courage is to look on untouched (unconcerned) when another suffers." It ended her romance with Nazi culture. As a 12-year-old, she had read *Gehanna*, a book in which a jailer, unable to bear his prisoners' sufferings, disappeared. Months later, a friend, carrying away a dying prisoner, was shocked to recognize him as the former jailer. He said, "It is harder to stand by and watch than to be with them and to share their suffering." That was how Ruth felt.

When Germany was divided after the war, her family was separated, and Ruth studied in an East German college. She lost her early interest in religion, and

No mountain too high

In her search for sufferers in remote mountains, Dr. Pfau once huddled for two days in a narrow valley, besieged and shot at by feuding mountain tribes. She jumped from rock to rock, clambering down steep slopes without climbing gear or ropes, just her helper instructing her to "Put your foot here … and here." She sat in a jeep as it was swept downstream by a raging, swollen river, and was carried over giddily swaying rope bridges across wide canyons, her eyes shut tightly. In war-torn Afghanistan, she and her team braved Kalaschnikov machine guns and Mujahadeen fire to cure patients.

But if she was afraid of heights, she was fearless when it came to dealing with tribal chiefs in a land where girls were killed by their brothers for returning a man's smile. When it came to curing her patients, Ruth Pfau tolerated no barriers of tradition.

She slept at night in the hut of a patient in a mountain desert, on a woven mat spread on the floor, after reading her Bible in Urdu by moonshine and candlelight. Wherever she and her team went in Pakistan, and since 1984 in Afghanistan, scores of the poor and neglected streamed in to have their pain relieved. Somehow, they knew when the doctor was in.

turned briefly to communism. Eventually, disillusioned and seeing no future in the east, she escaped in 1948 to join her publisher father in West Germany.

There, she studied internal medicine and obstetrics. She fell in love three times, the third for keeps, she thought. But her religious calling was stronger and, in 1957, she entered the order of The Daughters of the Heart of Maria.

TB cases and school From its humble hut, the Marie-Adelaide Leprosy Center has expanded under Dr. Pfau and her assistants. She sends out technicians to scout the remotest regions in Pakistan and Afghanistan for patients. Now, not just Hansen's disease but also tuberculosis cases are treated. With the help of a Belgian nun, she runs a rehabilitation center where patients learn a trade in order to earn a living. Outside Karachi, they run a school for 500 children.

True love In 1987, the woman who was sure she could not stay was made an honorary citizen of Pakistan. Her patients keep her there, the once hopeless abandoned girls squatting beside dung heaps and patients in need of surgery and transplants.

She meets courageous children, men, and women, who despite sufferings laugh and help each other. It gives her a tremendous sense of work that is meaningful and results that are tangible.

Marie-Elisabeth Lueders

"First Lady? I can't afford that. I'm the only man in the Free Democratic Party!" retorted the forceful 75-year-old, when she was named senior president of the German parliament on October 6, 1953. Almost 40 years earlier, when Marie-Elisabeth Lueders first attended a conference on population issues, the doormen and commissioners of the German Reichstag had tried to stop her as women were not yet allowed in parliament.

Politics at 12 Marie-Elisabeth was born on June 25, 1878. Her father was a privy counselor of the Cultural Ministry of Prussia, and many politicians and intellectuals, including the physicist Max Planck, were regular visitors to her home. By the time Marie-Elisabeth was 12, she was reading newspapers and parliamentary debates and burning to study at the college, closed to girls then. At 14, she picked up her courage to see the principal of the Technical High School. Kindly, but firmly, he told her, "This is not for girls. You wouldn't understand what's being taught here." She protested in vain that her brothers, who were planning to study at the school, were no smarter than she.

In 1901, she met members of the Federation of German Women's Associations and the inspiring activist for women's education, Helene Lange.

Their demands for women's rights to education and work sounded an echo in her hungry heart and mind, and she stayed a fervent feminist all her life.

Finally, at 31, in 1909, she began studying national economics and law at the Berlin University. Attending lectures was an unpleasant experience. Male students were insulting and they hooted and cheered when professors made snide remarks. It was hard for women students to find hostel rooms, and sometimes the police made surprise visits to check on their moral standing. In 1912, she graduated with a doctorate in political science. Her thesis angered the Prussian minister of trade for it sharply criticized the old-fashioned attitude of the authorities toward working women. It marked the start of many a change-stimulating provocation from the fiery Marie-Elisabeth.

"Just call me Major" From the beginning, till she was close to 80, Marie-Elisabeth Lueders had always had a problem-solving role. From 1912 to 1914, she worked as a housing administrator in the magistrate of Berlin-Charlottenburg, at a time where for the poor, she said, "a sleeping place couldn't even be described as a bed." She had to see to it that rooms were in a clean condition and well-aired and everyone had a bed. Fresh air was important but a problem, as children often fell out of windows. One day, as she approached, a little boy shouted up to the second floor, "Mum, open the windows! That long lady is coming!"

Later, she headed the welfare section of the Belgian Civil Administration for a year before being urgently called by the war ministry. Her help was required to organize women to run the industry and administration while the men were away at war. She held the rank of Major.

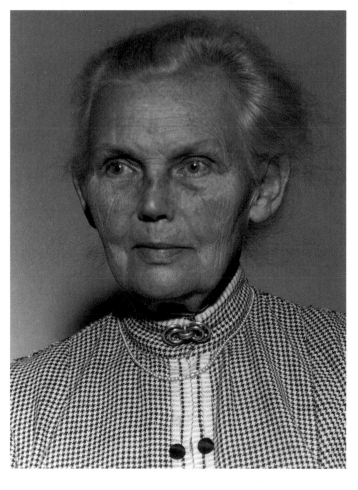

Marie-Elisabeth Leuders.

Too masculine to be human "Women must learn to want what society owes them and to demand what society owes them," she said. Realizing women could only be emancipated through political activity and not individual social work, she joined parliament in 1919 when women were granted suffrage rights.

With her fiery temperament and long experience of dealing with the authorities, she became a formidable mover of issues that included reform on citizenship rights and illegitimate children. She also opened up many jobs for women in the civil service. But political work is slow in bearing fruit. Thus her fight to remove the fault-finding clause in divorces only succeeded after 13 years. With Elisabeth Schwarzhaupt, she worked to remove the final-decision authority of husbands. It meant battling even women politicians, who declared firmly that the father was the head and the mother the heart of the family. Her passionate and eloquent speeches were full of sharp wit, humor, and plain truth. For her the world was "too masculine to be human."

On the edge of a knife She was arrested in 1937 by the Gestapo (Nazi secret service) for "malice and disloyalty." A storm of protests from international women's associations brought about her release four months later. Knowing the grave danger to herself, she nevertheless worked with a group of Quakers to help the politically persecuted and hid Jews in her house. Throughout the war, when, like millions of others, she lived a nomadic life, she found strength in the prayer, "Fear not, for I am with you."

80 and still shooting from the hip After the war, she was called back to take charge of social welfare as millions of refugees and returning war prisoners needed urgent help. In 1953, the FDP sent her to the federal parliament in Bonn. When she finally retired, Marie-Elisabeth Lueders was 82.

Why did she work so hard? Marie-Elisabeth felt that women should be active in overcoming discrimination themselves. Not one to mince words, she said, "Women who do not engage themselves in politics are political duds, and are no better than a piece of paper in the registration office."

The experience of two world wars made Marie-Elisabeth Lueders fight for peace. "Those who stay silent, agree," she said. With the help of Elisabeth Schwarzhaupt and Helene Weber, she freed German women from all military service and was shortlisted for the Nobel Peace Prize in 1960. Today, German women are not allowed to enlist for active military service, although they may join the army as administrators, doctors, or members of the military band.

Helene Lange

A stone flew through the window and the mob cheered. Just at that moment, in another house, a baby girl gave her first cry of life. Helene Lange was born on April 9, 1848, in the first glory of the revolution that had spilled over from France to Germany and broken down feudal structures. She was to become one of Germany's most significant women and would change the lives of women for a long time to come.

Education In the era of Helene's childhood, the 19th century, German girls were educated only so they would not bore their husbands. Helene, orphaned at 16, went to south Germany to live in a pastor's home for a year. There she met the educated society and felt very sharply the differences between the men and the less educated women, who were neither allowed or able to take part in intellectual discussions. She wanted to be a teacher, but her guardian in Oldenburg, her hometown, dismissed the idea as nonsense.

Hurdle jumping Not one to stumble over hurdles, Helene went to the Alsace as an *au pair* and educated herself privately. Then she took on a job as an educator before moving on to Berlin. There she met revolutionary women like Henrietta and Franziska Tibertius, who were fighting to work as doctors, and

Helene Lange.

read the works of Hedwig Dohm, a radical feminist, and Jeannette Schwerin, a pioneer fighter for the welfare state.

She took her teacher's exams and became a teacher, and later a principal who was very influential with her ideas on education for women. In 1890, she founded the General German Women Teachers' Association. In order to spread her ideas and concepts, she started a magazine, *Die Frau* (*The Woman*) in 1893, managing it with the help of her companion, colleague, and successor, Gertrud Baeumer, until her death. It became one of the most important organs of the middle-class feminist movement.

In Helene Lange's time, women teachers were more than a class below their male colleagues and only allowed to teach in private girls' schools. Women teachers, male German educators said, were totally incapable of thinking logically and were thus not capable of teaching mathematics or science. Helene Lange, who was a perspicacious and brilliant speaker, condemned this attitude. "The education of girls can simply not be left to men who openly express such low opinions of women," she said.

"Yellow" demands In 1887, together with women like Minna Cauer, she handed over a petition demanding a uniform education for boys and girls. As part of the petition, she added a "Yellow Brochure," detailing demands that included college-educated women teachers for girls. It caused an uproar and she was attacked severely by the press. A year later, parliament gave her a formal refusal. She proceeded to build her own school.

In 1889, financed by women's associations and the proceeds of fund-raising events, she started a *Realschule* ("RAY-ahl-shoo-le"), an intermediate secondary school to train women for jobs in commerce and industry. Four years later, the school was converted into a *Gymnasium* for girls. (In Germany, a *Gymnasium* is a school that prepares students for college.) The excellent results of the first graduates confirmed her belief that girls were as intelligent as boys. Her students had to study in foreign colleges, as German colleges were open to women only after 1901.

Before her death in 1930, Helene Lange was able to see the fruits of her work when women received political and legal rights and higher schooling for girls became widespread.

The sex debate Helene Lange was a very active feminist and the chairwoman of the General German Women's Association for 20 years. She was also a committee member of the Federation of German Women's Associations. Education was above all what she lived for, because she saw it as a vehicle of change for the emancipation of women. "Not the sex but the personality must decide," she said. Her target was middle-class, not working-class, women, but today girls of all classes have her and the other pioneers to thank, for education is the key to other gains.

Louise Otto-Peters

Was she "the lark of the women's movement" or "a prisoner of her class," as Clara Zetkin claimed? Louise Otto-Peters (1819–95) was no true revolutionary, yet she helped revolutionize the lives of women.

For a bite of black bread Louise Otto's upbringing strongly colored her life. She was brought up to be decent and feminine, yet aware of political happenings. "Read," her father instructed, "so you don't sit there dumbly when there is talk of current affairs and you have to feel ashamed of yourself."

Her parents instilled in her a deep sense of social justice, and her poems, books, and newspaper articles often had social or political themes. When she saw the difference between the working class and rich factory owners, she poured her outrage into books and poems. In "Songs of a German Girl," she wrote about the misery of home workers who labored "pale cheeked, red eyed ... for a bite of black bread." She sent fiery reports to royal commissions about the situation.

The lark During the early days of the 1848 revolution of France that spilled over to Germany, leading to uprisings against the monarchy everywhere, there was a sense of spiritual liberty. The influence of freedom fighters like

Louise Otto-Peters.

Robert Blum came through in her poems and she was called the "Lark of the People's Spring."

Louise wanted to use this momentum to keep up women's interest in public life through education. She felt that "... Participation in the interests of the state is not just a right but a duty of women ...," and marriages of convenience for women were out of date. Though only 17 when her parents died, she did not allow herself to be "protected" by a male, preferring to lead an independent life, even though it brought her great criticism.

"Lex Otto-Peters" When a minister called a commission to look into labor conditions, she sent her "Address of a German girl," demanding better working opportunities for women. She pointed out the moral danger of women whose low earnings forced them into prostitution. The address made her a public figure. To influence changes for women, Louise began publishing a journal in 1849. _Frauen-Zeitung_ (_Women's Journal_) reported on social conditions and called for women to work together. To the German authorities this was the last straw. In 1850, a press law, popularly known as Lex Otto-Peters, banned women from editorial work. She moved to another state but finally had to close down her journal in 1852.

A fleeting love At 39, she married journalist and freedom fighter August Peters, after his release from prison. She helped him with the publication of a democratic journal until his death just six years later.

Truly womanly In 1865, together with Auguste Schmidt and Henriette Goldschmidt, she founded the General German Women's Association in Leipzig. "The women must take things into their own hands," she said. It helped that she was seen as moderate and "truly womanly," for women could join the Association without fear of condemnation. The mother of a schoolteacher, Auguste Schmidt, told her daughter, "Under Louise Otto, you can go ahead and join the fight." Women were afraid of being called "emancipated" as it had sexual overtones then. What they wanted was emancipation in the areas of work and education. In keeping with the very conservative upbringing of women then, the Association did not call for political rights. This was left to more radical groups.

Until her death at 76, Louise Otto-Peters was convinced that "In all we aim to achieve, we must never deny our femininity." Under her, the Association fought for and got better education and training for girls, more work for women in the civil service and other fields, and rights over their own property. Later, these advances paved the way for further improvements. Through being non-radical about women's roles in a very conservative time—not battling for rights but gaining them through loyal service, and not criticizing society but adapting to it—she and her co-emancipators were able to draw many supporters from the middle class and so set the wheels turning for greater emancipation for German women.

Clara Zetkin

Clara Eissner (1857–1933) was set early on the path of a revolutionary. Her mother inspired her with the ideals of the middle-class women's movement, and her teacher father encouraged her sympathy with the revolution of 1848. As a young teacher, Clara met Ossip Zetkin, a Russian emigré whose strong influence brought her into contact with socialist thinkers in Zurich and Paris. She took on Zetkin's name without marrying him as she did not wish to lose her German citizenship. In Paris, they lived on the edge of poverty, she with the dual burden of children and work. She had to bring up their two sons singlehandedly as Ossip died early.

Stirring up the masses In 1889, Clara made such a strong stand for women at a meeting of the socialist movement that it agreed to accept the cause of working women and girls.

Two years after her return to Germany, she was made the editor of *Die Gleichheit* (*Equality*). The biweekly journal represented not only women's interests, but was a mouthpiece of the socialist movement. It became her work for 25 years and, through it, she became a leading figure in the working women's

Clara Zetkin urging the masses toward revolution.

movement. At that time, working women accepted their poor work conditions passively. With the help of other women, Clara agitated for change and improvement. Women were soon banned from political meetings, and there were clashes with the police. Still, the brave women continued, fired on by Clara Zetkin.

> "My life is the life of the party, of the revolutionary proletariat vanguard, and that is not pleasant. I stand as a soldier of the revolution at my post and will endure."
> —*Clara Zetkin*

Us and them Clara Zetkin pointed out the differences between middle-class women's associations, for whom "work was a duty, an honor, and a right," and working-class women's associations, for whom work was "a cruel compulsion." The former were fighting for social equality within their own class, while the workers were fighting together with men against the class system.

Spitfire peace-seeker Like her close friend, Rosa Luxemburg (see page 24), Clara Zetkin was a strong follower of the socialists Marx and Engels, and later of Lenin. She attacked members of the Social Democratic Party who wanted to cooperate with capitalists, and consequently she was excluded from the party committee in 1908.

A fervent pacifist, Clara organized an international anti-war demonstration (ignoring a ban by her party) and published leaflets, for which she was arrested for treason. Her supporters protested and she was released. In 1917, she left the Social Democratic Party to join the Independents, and the SDP promptly fired her as editor of *Die Gleichheit*. Later, she joined the German Communist Party where she built up the women's wing and published a journal, *The Communist Woman*.

Superwoman on crutches Clara Zetkin took part in at least 300 assemblies a year, apart from writing books and articles for journals. She also worked for the German Communist Party and the International Communist Party, and was president of the Red Cross and a member of the Reichstag. She had always been in poor health, and it worsened with age so that she often collapsed while giving speeches at congresses. Later, she had to walk on crutches and was nearly blind, but she had an iron will. In the last year of her life, though 75 and weak, she travelled from Moscow to Germany to open parliament in Berlin; she was its honorary president.

In spite of jeers and taunts, she made a passionate appeal for resistance against the Nazis. When the "soldier of the revolution" died in Archangelskoje near Moscow, more than 600,000 Russians attended her funeral, and she was buried at the Kremlin walls.

Johanna Kirchner

Frankfurt remembers Johanna Kirchner (1889–1944), the German social democrat, welfare worker, and resistance fighter, with fondness and pride. There is a Johanna Kirchner Street. A home, a foundation, and a bookshop also bear her name.

A family tradition Johanna, the eldest of six children, was born into a Hessian family with a long socialist background. Her grandfather was the first town councilor of Frankfurt, who during Chancellor Bismarck's time was deported through anti-socialist laws. Throughout 12 years of persecution, Johanna's grandmother used to wrap the party flag around her body whenever a house search was anticipated. Johanna's father, a master joiner, was a dedicated social democrat.

Johanna became involved in the workers' cause at 14, when she joined the Socialist Workers' Youth Organization. She worked as a reporter for party and union congresses and was active in the women's emancipation movement, fighting for their social equality and better labor protection laws. She remained active even after her marriage to Karl Kirchner, a technician who became a journalist because of lung problems.

When German women got the right to vote, many women politicians turned to welfare work. Johanna was active in unions and welfare work. She helped the Social Democratic Party member of parliament, Maria Juchacz, found the *Arbeiterwohlfahrt* (Workers' Welfare) in 1919. She had an especially soft spot for children, and during strikes, when workers were locked out, she organized the "adoption" of workers' children by Frankfurt families. During the war and the inflation that followed, she brought undernourished and sick German children to Switzerland to recuperate.

Johanna Kirchner.

Keeping the same shirt on Johanna was one of those in the Social Democratic Party who did not "change shirts" when the Nazis came to power. Her husband was interrogated several times between 1933 and 1945, and he died from the effects of torture six months after war ended. Johanna herself organized activities in support of arrested party members and helped victims of political persecution to leave Germany until she was discovered in 1933. Her daughters, Lotte and Inge, urged her to flee.

Hidden pain At this time, the Social Democratic Party, the German Communist Party, and the trade unions were already banned. The Saar area—which was then under the administration of the League of Nations and not the Nazis—became a haven for many refugees until, two years later, the Germans took the state back under their wing. Johanna had found a refuge there, working in her party office and at a restaurant of the Workers' Welfare founder, Maria Juchacz.

> "Nursing, advice and hands-on help was needed. Women like Hanna were born for that, although she herself was not created for such a hard life of exile. Her thoughts and feelings were with her family, her loving children, or her Frankfurt ... She could only hide (her pain) by caring for others."
>
> —*Maria Juchacz*

Escape and capture When the Saar was overrun by the Nazis, Johanna fled to Forbach in France to work in the resistance movement and with refugees. She organized help and gathered information for other refugees, German volunteers in the Spanish Civil War, and members of the German underground resistance. She helped publish a journal, the *Saarnachrichten*, that condemned Nazis. Through exact and analytical reports on the situation at home and on the resistance front, she not only kept German leaders in exile in Prague and London informed, but also offered suggestions on what should be done. When war broke out, she was arrested and interned in a French concentration camp.

In 1942, she was handed over to the Gestapo, tortured and interrogated, before being sentenced to 10 years' imprisonment. The infamous president of the "People's Court," Dr. Roland Freisler, was dissatisfied. He demanded a re-trial. Under his chairmanship, it was a farce. He shouted at the judges, "Don't let yourself be misled by the seeming good impression of the accused. I will show her daughters what kind of a mother they have."

She was sentenced to death as a traitor and decapitated on June 9, 1944, in Berlin. Germany lost another of the thousands of courageous women who died for their convictions.

Monika Griefahn

Greenpeace and Monika Griefahn ... it was love at first hearing. She was then organizing a seminar in France and "Greenpeace" spelt courage, ideas, and idealism. "I have never lived as intensively. We planned and discussed actions at the kitchen table and the phone rang day and night."

When the workload got too heavy, she gave up her job to become full-time manager for Greenpeace Germany, for half her old salary. Later, she became one of five international directors of Greenpeace International. The next few years saw her globetrotting, planning,

and actively taking part in spectacular Greenpeace actions. Diving in the path of ships carrying spent acids, chemicals, and nuclear waste; dumping rotten fish in front of chemical concerns and public institutions; and lobbying for whales and seals to prevent their slaughter kept her adrenaline pumping for the thousands of other hours spent behind desks and at conferences.

Kicking up dust for a better world Born on October 3, 1954, the eldest of four daughters, Monika Griefahn has never stopped being in the thick of action, whether as a girl guide, class president,

Monika Griefahn on a boat during a Greenpeace campaign.

Monika Griefahn, the minister of the environment who believes in solving problems through frequent discussion, walks the streets to talk to the people.

or provocative school newspaper writer. After co-founding an Amnesty International Group, she organized youth activities in Germany and France, collected donations for Chilean refugees, demonstrated against nuclear energy, helped found feminist bookshops, and was part of many citizens' initiatives.

"I suppose being active in groups gave me what I missed at home—companionship and a forum for my ideas," she said. At home, nobody could understand the cauldron of fiery ideas bubbling in her head.

Calculated risks and preparedness

After her maiden speech as an Amnesty International member, Monika was criticized by her group for reading off her paper and not being well prepared. But now the legendary German perfection is clear in her work. Before actions are undertaken, groundwork and research are thoroughly prepared and solutions looked for. "Before we jump in the paths of ships, we train for weeks in advance so we know exactly what the risks are."

Marriage and motherhood

In 1986, she married Michael Braungart, manager of the Institute for Environment in Hamburg and an expert in toxic waste management. In 1988, their son Jonas was born, and after he had seen America, Russia, and Australia with his parents, they decided he needed a stable home with other children to play with.

While on the lookout for an alternative job, Monika was offered the post of minister of the environment in Lower Saxony, although she belongs to no political party. She hesitated, not wanting to be an "alibi" woman (a token woman chosen to win women's votes or for publicity). Michael encouraged her to take the job, and subsequently he did the cooking and took Jonas to and from the childcare center.

"When I am home, I devote all my time to my son. It's better to be a happy part-time mother than an unhappy full-time one," she said. Criticized for canceling important appointments at short notice, she pointed out that sometimes her duties as a mother are more important. "Here you have the situation of a woman in real life," she beamed at her critics.

Politics Monika Griefahn has an utter distaste for the rabidly personal attacks of politicians, preferring rational negotiations and logical, subject-related arguments. In cabinet meetings, women ministers generally do not command as much attention and respect as their male colleagues. Within her own ministry, a traditionally male-oriented department with engineers and scientists, she has had to work hard to win the acceptance of staff who are probably more used to cautious and docile women.

Round Table style "Previously we fought for politicians to act on our demands. Now I have the chance to act myself." Still, it is no easy task and Monika Griefahn has to take being fired on from both sides in her stride.

She has a collaborative and democratic style. "We discuss things rationally and decide on the best course of action together." Her Round Table project to bring together people with conflicting interests in the search for satisfactory solutions to environmental problems is typical of her style.

Toilet cleaner and fairy godma Because of her engagement in Greenpeace, people expect her to wander through the land with a magic wand in her hand. She compares her job to that of a toilet lady who has to clean away other people's dirt. The list of tasks

is long. But even experts praise the firm and effective way she confronts the problems of reducing rubbish and the number of regulations on air and water pollution she has pushed through since entering office in June 1990. Monika is still tackling wastefulness and pollution on land, in the water and the air, and fighting for national parks, compostable packaging, and renewable energy from the sun and wind.

The future of the children Monika Griefahn is one minister who encourages and applauds public demonstrations like those against nuclear energy. When the federal minister of the environment announced plans to store nuclear waste in an underground tunnel at Salzgitter (nearly 2 million cubic feet of radioactive waste had by then been accumulated from the 20 nuclear power stations in Germany and the search for new storage space was growing desperate), Monika Griefahn led opposition to this proposal. She was determined that Lower Saxony should not be the victim. The mother voiced the people's conviction when she said, "I am fighting for the future of our children."

"Women find it easier to take a moral stand. Men often want a rational reason to do something like fighting against pollution of the sea. All we need is our common sense."
—*Monika Griefahn*

Marlene Dietrich

She was "not a person to be judged by normal rules," said her daughter, Maria Riva. Indeed, Germany's best known actress outside Germany, Marlene Dietrich, born Marie Magdalene (1901–92), played the vamp to perfection and loved to shock. Even in the 1920s, when Berlin was a "moral curiosity," she was very extravagant, and people would

stand to stare or run after her when she walked along the fashionable shopping alleys. She always managed to look seductive, whether in slinky gowns, with her father's monocle stuck in her eye, or in trousers.

Marie Magdalene's mother taught her daughter that life was no bed of roses, paid for her violin lessons, and made her take cold showers to harden herself. She also gave her a love of classical books. At 19, Marie Magdalene worked as a showgirl at night and sold gloves by day, took dance lessons and even joined a boxing club to keep fit. As her mother disapproved of her show life, she shortened her name to Marlene. Her Prussian officer father, whom she remembered as smelling of leather and horses, had died when she was 9.

Her unmistakable aloof, long-legged, sleek look was groomed by Josef von Sternberg, who took her to Hollywood. There she acted in the movie, *The Blue Angel*, as the unforgettable Lola-Lola. Von Sternberg was the father she never had, and he made her a superstar, one of the top earners in Hollywood. While she led a life of great extravagance and luxury, "at work she was a soldier," said movie director Billy Wilder, "… highly disciplined and always helpful."

In spite of her glamor, she was very down to earth and there was a strong *Hausfrau* hidden in her. She would think nothing of putting on an apron and

washing dishes, tying a man's shoelaces, or cooking something for him. When someone was sick, she played nurse. Once, during a tour, caught scrubbing the floor by a reporter, she joked, "I am the queen of Ajax!"

Germany tried to woo her back to make propaganda movies for the Nazis in 1936, but she refused. Instead, in 1938, she became an American citizen and a symbol of free Germany, and made anti-Nazi broadcasts in German. She entertained American troops all over Europe, often risking her life, and financed the escape of Jewish friends. Some Germans neither understood nor forgave her for entertaining American troops during the war, but the United States gave Marlene Dietrich its highest civilian honor: the Medal of Freedom.

In 1953, at 52, she began a new career as a cabaret artist, singing and dancing on stage. For 20 years, she toured the world as a one-woman entertainer. At 72, the amazing woman gave a television gala performance. She retired only after she broke her leg in Sydney.

Among Marlene Dietrich's many films are *Morocco* (1930), *Dishonored* (1931), *Shanghai Express* (1932), *Blonde Venus, The Devil Is A Woman, The Garden Of Allah, The Scarlet Empress, A Foreign Affair* (1948), and *Witness For The Prosecution* (1958).

Opposite and above: Marlene Dietrich.

chapter six

A Lifetime

Clothes often signal changes in a society. A glance at German schools shows that almost everyone is in jeans. Skirts and dresses are a rare sight. It speaks of a new freedom in the society and changes in the roles and lifestyles of women that go beyond leisure and fashion.

While tradition and ceremony still form a corset for German society, there is an almost visible snapping of old fetters, and many customs have been thrown overboard for a more hectic way of life.

Birth

Fewer children seems to be the trend. The birth rate is 1.5 and dropping.

Long ago, when Germans believed the expectant mother and her unborn child needed extra special protection, she was armed with amulets and crosses, prayers and blessed items; keyholes were sealed and doors kept shut to prevent witches from sneaking in.

Opposite and right: German mothers form strong bonds with their children from the very beginning, thanks to the generous maternity leave allowances required by law.

Today, a German baby is usually born in a modern hospital and, with the ultrasound scanning machine, even its sex is no surprise. Germans have folk ways of predicting the baby's sex. If it is overdue, it has to be a girl as she's keeping everyone waiting while she makes herself pretty, and if the baby is conceived at full moon, a boy is expected. A lively baby, they say, is a future soccer player.

Above: A baby is blessed at the baptism font.

Opposite: A midwife washes a newborn baby in earlier times.

On birthdays, name days, First Communion, confirmation, and on other festive occasions, girls were given presents meant for their marriage by relatives and godparents—a piece of a cutlery set, a collector's item like a coffee or tea cup and saucer with gilded edges. Other gifts are parade cushions (put on top of pillows for day decoration), linens, crocheted, towels, and initialed handkerchiefs. These days, jewelry, books, purses, watches, and money are more typical and appreciated gifts.

Christian ceremonies

As most Germans are either Catholics or Protestants, childhood rites are Christian. They are the same for girls and boys.

Baptism At the baptism ceremony that usually takes place when the baby is a few weeks to a few months old, he or she becomes a member of the church. To wash away sins, the priest or pastor pours some water over the baby's forehead, a procedure that causes a lusty yell. The baby's mother is usually blessed, too. In the old days, many mothers died giving birth and the blessing was to thank God for her health.

Two or more godparents chosen earlier are present, one of whom will carry the baby, who is dressed in a lacy white baptism gown. Traditionally, they take care of the child's moral and religious upbringing till the age of 14 or 15, when the child is confirmed, or till marriage. Their role is becoming more that of reliable present givers, especially if they live far away. The ceremony is followed by a day-long family celebration.

First Communion Around the age of 8 or 9, Catholic children prepare for their first Holy Communion with about six months of extra catechism lessons. It is an important ceremony and relatives attend to observe it.

Historical rites

Baptism has been a Christian ceremony for centuries and the tradition and customs accompanying it used to be full of superstition that is mostly forgotten today. In East Prussia, for example, the mother and the guests had to cross over an axe and a broom laid at the church threshold to block off evil spirits who feared metal (represented by the axe) and the kindling of life (represented by the broom). Eggs, a fertility symbol, were often given by friends and relatives to bring luck and blessings.

Before the Middle Ages, a newborn child's life was less important than the mother's. During the Middle Ages, the church decided that a child had to be born alive in order for it to be baptized; in critical situations the mother's life was sacrificed and the baby removed by cesarean section. Midwives risked being blamed when things went wrong, for example, if the baby was deformed.

If there were already many daughters in the family, the father could refuse a baby girl. A bad omen or dream could cause the same reaction to a baby boy. The word for midwife is *Hebamme* ("HAYB-am-meh"), from the old Germanic *Hevianna*, meaning "the lifter." It comes from the ceremony where the midwife lifted the child from the floor on the orders of the father and handed it to him. If he took the baby, it was accepted and allowed to live. The child was then given a name and water was poured over it. The last part of the ceremony is partially found again in the Christian baptism.

Virgins as luck bringers Cults arose in the early days when conditions were harsh and people were close to nature. While boys were preferred to carry on the family line, the innocence of young girls was believed to rejuvenate the old, heal illness, and stimulate the

productivity of nature. Virgins pulled the plough ceremoniously over fields, and the cloth for sowing grains had to be woven by a girl aged no more than 7. In a drought, farmers pushed young girls in carts into a stream and pulled them home backwards into the village, all the while making the sign of the cross and calling out to the Nordic god of thunder, Thor.

Birth trees A tree was sometimes planted after the birth of a child, and this custom was related to its well-being in some mysterious way. Pear trees were planted for girls and apple trees for boys. In some areas, the *Thuja occidentalis*, called the Tree of Life in German, was planted by the father after the birth of a boy.

On the first Sunday after Easter, girls go to church dressed like little brides in white dresses that symbolize innocence, with a garland, and a veil or ribbons in their hair. Boys wear a black or dark blue suit, or an elegant windbreaker, jacket, or cardigan they can use again. In some rural areas children wear traditional costumes. Before the ceremony, children confess their sins to a priest and receive absolution (forgiveness).

They enter the church carrying a rosary and a candle. During Mass, they receive the host, a wafer of unleavened bread symbolizing the body of Christ. After Mass, breakfast is served in the parish rooms as the children have had to fast before Communion. A grand lunch at home or a restaurant is followed by coffee and cakes in the afternoon and an elaborate cold supper in the evening.

Holy Communion group photo with a priest.

Teen years

At 14, teenagers are permitted by law to choose their own religion and to withdraw from religious lessons at school. The confirmation ceremony is usually held after this "age of choice." A few generations ago, it not only marked their full acceptance into the church, but also the end of compulsory schooling and the start of job apprenticeship.

Confirmation   At 14 or 15, Protestant children reconfirm the faith that they were too young to appreciate at baptism. During a worship service between Easter and Pentecost, they receive a special blessing and are accepted into the church as full members. They have the right to take part in the full Holy Communion. Girls wear a dark blue or black outfit, sometimes with a white blouse. They are given Bibles or hymnbooks as presents. This is another big family affair that relatives and godparents attend.

Catholics have a similar confirmation ceremony, known as *Firmung* ("FEER-moong"), which is seen as a continuation of the baptism ceremony. This rite is normally performed by the bishop or his representative, who lays his hands on the child and anoints the forehead by rubbing it with chrism, a blessed oil. The Catholic family celebration for confirmation is on a smaller scale than for the First Communion.

Waltz and lambada Dancing is on the agenda when Germans reach 15. Not only do they whirl and squash toes through ballroom and disco steps, they are also given lessons in chivalry and etiquette. No true German girl or boy will skip this rite of passage. The entire school class attends the course together.

The basic course ends in a party. Girls are given corsages and boys a small gift. Sons and daughters, dressed to the nines, also dance with their parents. Many a tear is shed by mothers, and less openly by fathers, on this evening that marks another step out of the nest.

Regulations Germany has strict laws for teenagers. The age of majority is 18. At 16, they are allowed to smoke and drink wine or beer in public and to stay out till midnight unaccompanied by an adult. The curfew for those below 16 is 10 p.m. But as discos and parties are weekend highlights for teenagers, and the action takes place close to midnight, time, age, and drink limits are forgotten under cover of the night and heavy make-up. Youth pubs are also a popular meeting ground. Girls usually have to persuade their parents to relax the curfew while boys have fewer problems.

Dancing at a church convention for teenagers.

Group activities during the teen years pave the way for individual dating.

criticize their parents' habits, like using insecticides or not recycling.

Youth and sports clubs, churches, and other groups organize many activities and outings for teenagers. Like their parents, young Germans love traveling, and girls often do so in groups, using the cheap train passes for young travelers all over Europe, or cycling and camping. Schools organize school exchange trips for a few weeks each year to France, England, or other countries.

Traditional roles In bringing up their children, many modern parents try to avoid sexual differentiation. This is less the case in smaller towns and rural areas.

Fathers tend to be more tradition-bound than mothers on this point. For them, baby girls should still be taught to be lovable and tender, clean and obedient, and boys, strong and active, independent and manly.

Although tradition has been watered down, the upbringing of girls still reflects their future role as housewives. From 6 to 9 years of age, boys and girls are expected to help equally in housework, yet girls do more cleaning and babysitting, and boys more fetching, repairing, and gardening.

As they grow older, girls are given more housework than boys. They still choose jobs that enable them to balance career and family, whereas boys look for big money.

Encouraged by peer pressure, girls may be experimenting with sex at this time. With better sex education in school, this tendency has been reduced. Girls spend a lot of time with each other, but also move around in mixed groups. Many smoke and drink to express independence. Drug-taking has spread to schools, and parents are warned to look out for signs of children going astray.

Fashion, music, boys, discos, and sports interest German girls most at this stage. Many are also active in charity and church work, cultural programs, or environmental groups. Today, they are highly aware of issues concerning the environment, and often observe and

Education

Several decades ago, a formal education for girls prepared them mainly for their future role as housewives. Today, they are trained for work outside the home.

A sugary start Schooling may start with kindergarten, when the child is 3 and toilet-trained. When she turns 6, she goes to elementary school. On the first day she brings a huge, colorful cone filled with sweets, fruit, and nuts. This is meant to sweeten the seriousness of life to come. Elementary schoolchildren go to neighborhood schools. Since many of them walk to school, one of the first lessons they receive is how to cross a road safely. Drivers who see children standing at the roadside holding out an arm have to stop for them to cross.

Great emphasis is placed on neatly written school work and discipline in the classroom, although sociologists say girls are expected to be more obedient than boys. Children are generally expected by German adults to be quiet and well behaved. In smaller towns or neighborhoods, young children will greet passers-by, even total strangers, with a polite "Good day."

Co-education Except for some schools run mainly by churches, German schools have been coed for more than 20 years. The aim is to give girls and boys natural everyday contact with each other, remove old role-casting, and promote a cooperative spirit early in life. Experience has shown, however, that the old role-casting has not changed.

In courses for traditionally "male" subjects like science and computer studies, the more aggressive boys dominate. Girls are guided into languages and the humanities, and boys into science and technical subjects. Pupils in all-girl schools are said to be less

The sugar cone sweetens the first day of elementary school.

The school system

Elementary education lasts four to six years, the period varying with each state. Pupils are then streamed into one of three main types of middle school.

The *Hauptschule* ("HOWPT-shoo-le") is a general secondary school up to the 9th or 10th grade, when pupils are 15 or 16. Pupils go on to vocational training, but some states also offer intermediate certificates in the 10th grade. The *Realschule* ("RAY-ahl-shoo-le") is an intermediate secondary school that takes pupils to 10th grade and prepares them for practical work as well as for more advanced vocational or technical colleges. The *Gymnasium* that ends at the 13th grade with an *Abitur* certificate entitles the pupil to a college education. It is not uncommon for an *Abitur* student to take up an apprenticeship in a practical job before attending college, while others go straight into working life.

The *Gesamtschule* ("Ger-SAHMT-shoo-le") or comprehensive school combines all forms, and pupils are not streamed till the 10th grade.

hampered and free to develop according to individual inclination. Graduates of all-girl schools form the majority of the girls in technical, science, and information technology courses at colleges, as well as in science competitions for youths. This observation has led some educators to call for a return to separate schools.

Apprenticeship This is part of an excellent system that gives young Germans job training. To be accepted into a particular profession, a pupil has to apply for an apprenticeship posting at various companies. Training is given voluntarily by companies, and they usually train more apprentices than they themselves need. It is a traditional duty of German business to produce a pool of qualified labor for the economy.

The trainee—the *Auszubildende* ("OWS-tzu-bil-dehn-de") or *Azubi* for short—studies theory once or twice a week or several weeks full-time at a vocational school. At the same time, he or she gets on-the-job training at a private or public company that pays a training wage.

The majority of girls prefer training as clerks, dental and medical assistants, hairdressers, and salesgirls. Many employers are reluctant to accept girls into traditionally male jobs in manufacturing or mechanics. This is why more girls than boys fail to find an apprenticeship and are more likely to be unemployed or have a lower income and poorer job prospects. More girls than boys do full-time vocational schooling, especially if they cannot find an apprenticeship vacancy. But schooling cannot replace practical experience, which is still required at the end of the course to round off their education.

In the past, girls chose jobs with shorter training so they could start earning earlier and marry younger. Today, they opt for longer job training and higher education.

College Education and qualification are no longer the reasons why women lag behind in position, work opportunities, or income. Nearly half the college student population are women, most of whom study the arts, languages, social work, and teaching, but there is a strong trend toward medicine, law, business studies, and economics. A minority study engineering, mathematics, and physics, and fewer study electrical engineering and machine construction. This situation is reflected in the teaching staff; more women lecture in arts than science courses. In the former East Germany, since the 1980s, half the students were women who studied economics, teaching, literature, and language. About 27.9% studied engineering.

College courses last an average of four years, while courses in specialized colleges called *Fachhochschule* ("Fakh-hokh-shoo-le") last three to four years. Most German students spend on average six years at college or four years at a *Fachhochschule*, graduating later than many college students elsewhere.

Women at a college lecture.

The *Abitur* prank

Germans have a saying: "After the hard slogging it is time to let the sow out." After the *Abitur* or college entrance exams, the class usually plays an *Abi-streich* ("AHBEE-strai-sh"), a prank to prevent lessons from taking place and to leave their mark in the school records.

Pupils stay up all night taping or boarding up doors and windows, building stacks of straw at the school entrance, or sealing the school gate with bricks and mortar. A teacher's car may be taken apart and reassembled in the classroom. Lessons can start only after the teachers have removed all barricades, and this usually means the school has a day off.

Some classes conduct a mock trial during which their teacher's crimes are read out. The verdict by a jury of pupils never varies from "guilty," and the sentence is a harmless punishment like a bucket of water poured over the teacher's head. The *Abi* class publishes a school paper in which the teachers are taken apart with scathing wit. The final celebration is a prom night.

Laboratory assistant in Leverkusen.

Work

The family is no longer the sole focus of German women's lives, and working is a planned phase. Almost all single women have a job. Social contact, challenge, fulfillment, recognition, interesting activities, money, and independence—all these draw women to the work place.

In rural areas, girls who are unable to find a job often work in households and on family farms, as unemployment is seen as a disgrace and due to sheer laziness.

Women's work At the work place, women are still climbing over hurdles. They generally have poorer work conditions, incomes, and opportunities for promotion than men. Equal pay for equal work has long been law, but it has not been realized in all sectors, whether for unskilled workers, computer specialists, or doctors. Women are said to have lower incomes because of lower qualifications, and shorter years of work because they leave for family reasons. However, in many jobs women have to be more qualified than men for the same position, and yet they are often paid less.

Many German women also work in lower paying industries like the textile industry. Industries pay extra for work needing muscle power, but not for work needing nimble fingers. In the civil service, however, equal pay is the rule.

Rosier times In the early 1980s, most female industrial workers had only on-the-job training, if they had training at all. They also tended to be pushed into monotonous jobs. The situation has changed as people have begun to recognize the importance of education and training.

At the same time, more powerful positions are being given to women whose awareness of women's inferior position is coupled with a desire to effect improvements. When jobs are scarce, women become competitors, but in times of economic expansion when jobs are abundant, women have the best chances of making a headway. Germany has had boom years for more than a decade. It has been a time of greater partnership between men and women.

> **A new job is a significant occasion. A new employee has to give colleagues in the department an *Einstand* ("EIN-stahnd") within a few weeks of starting work. (The opposite is *Ausstand*, for those who leave.) During a breakfast break, the new colleague brings or buys coffee and fresh rolls filled with cheese and cold cuts. Beer or wine may be served if the employer permits alcohol. With the *Einstand*, the newcomer is officially established and accepted.**

Marriage

Emancipation has not nudged out love and family instincts. Although some prefer to remain single or not to have children, most women still wish to have a family. In the past, women had to wait for men to initiate the romance and to propose. Now they are also active in the search for partners. Work, school, and recreation places serve as contact points, but newspaper advertisements and marriage institutes are also popular means of finding partners.

A few decades ago, cohabitation was a great disgrace, but it is now very commonplace. Many couples live together and decide to marry only when the woman is expecting a child. German psychologists say that in such an arrangement, the woman is more independent than a wife, does less housework, and talks more about equality with her partner.

When wedding bells do finally ring, most Germans still celebrate marriage with pomp and tradition, although some modern couples prefer to do away with the trimmings. The average marriage age for German women is about 25 years.

The wedding Following the civil ceremony at the *Standesamt* ("STAHN-dehs-ahmt") or courthouse, there is usually a church ceremony. A few generations ago, brides wore black with a white veil while farm daughters had

Wedding customs

Wedding customs vary from place to place in Germany, and more are observed in rural areas than in towns. The reasons for most of them have been forgotten.

A smashing bash An informal party called *Polterabend* ("POL-ter-AH-behnd") takes place at the bride's house on the eve of the civil ceremony. It is an open house for all friends and neighbors. Guests bring crockery and start smashing it at the entrance in an age-old custom of scaring evil spirits from the bride's house. Today, evil spirits are not acknowledged, so Germans say "fragments bring luck." Long ago, only stoneware or porcelain (old plates, cups, and jugs) would do for breaking; glass, a symbol of joy, was a bad omen. Today, however, not only glass, but also tissue or toilet paper, and styrofoam are thrown by some instead of porcelain.

At around midnight, the couple sweeps away the pieces, while guests try to make it difficult for them to do so. Sweeping against odds represents the couple's fight against the problems life brings. For the guests it is an evening of great fun and relaxation, with hilarious poems being composed about the couple and read aloud.

Circles In some areas, at the stroke of 12 on the wedding night, the bride is circled by unmarried women and the groom by bachelors. Married guests break up the circles and build one circle, symbolizing that two are now one.

The circle is a recurring symbol. In the past, it was believed to have the power to exclude evil and preserve wholeness. It was also a traditional way of announcing the bride's virtue: closed garlands symbolized virginity. Until recently, village priests made sure the correct headdress was worn. In Schwalm, a groom who had had illegitimate children was only allowed to wear his elaborate headgear on his head at an angle!

Ransom for the bride In another custom, the bride is kidnapped during the evening celebration and held at an inn (a small hotel, usually with a pub). The groom and some friends have to travel from inn to inn in search of her, buying a round of drinks at each stop. Unless the groom has a friend to stand in for him at the drinking sessions, he will be quite drunk by the time he finds his bride. This is probably just as well, for he is presented with a bill for the expenses of the "kidnappers," which represents the "ransom" or purchase price for his bride.

The ransom game is a reminder that a marriage used to be more than a union between two people. It united two families, villages, or farms through a contract that involved ambition, greed, village peace, and safety. Many couples reject this custom as it disrupts the party and, besides, the police deal most severely with drunk drivers.

colorful costumes reflecting their status and property. Today the bride usually wears a white wedding gown and the groom, a black suit, white shirt and tie.

During the ceremony, vows and rings are exchanged. Sometimes, the groom's colleagues or sporting club friends form a guard of honor at the church entrance. Chimney sweeps in black uniform and ladders may line the entrance, or firemen in uniform form an arc of spouting water.

Friends may play pranks on the couple, like placing a plastic stork with a baby dangling from its bill on the chimney of their new house, or hanging a line of tiny baby clothes high up across the road. Some go to extremes like wrapping the entire house in toilet paper.

Wedding dinners are attended by relatives and close friends.

Splitting the bill Dowries are no longer paid, and etiquette varies about whose parents foot the bills for the celebration. Many couples now pay themselves. Traditionally, the girl's parents pay for the food, bridal dress, floral decor, and bridal bouquet, and the groom's parents may pay for the drinks. The bride provides her own trousseau (linen and crockery), most of which has been collected throughout her life, while the groom provides the rest. Today, as more people marry late, many would have been living alone as singles and two sets of everything are already available.

Left: Women working in the house or garden is a common sight in Germany.

Opposite: At midnight, the couple clears up the mess of smashed crockery.

The honeymoon is over Nowadays, women expect greater partnership in marriage, but they usually still do the housework.

Older women tend to be more duty-bound toward their family and partner. Even those working will rush home after work, and by the time the husband is home, the house is clean and a hot meal is on the table.

Working-class families are more traditional in this respect than the upper middle class. German women are legendary homemakers, and many a proud housewife can claim her floor is clean enough to eat off.

Every day a working day A mother is expected to be always there for her children, especially when they are very young. Most schoolchildren come home from school around noon to a hot lunch. She usually supervises their homework, and afternoons are often spent bringing them to music lessons, school games, medical appointments, or shopping. Through their children, many women also have greater contact with each other.

One favorite activity of mother and child is *basteln* ("BAHS-teln") where they make toys and other objects of daily use. Since labor costs are high, handicraft is a valued traditional skill most German women master from early childhood and pass on to their children.

In the former East Germany, most mothers worked full-time while the state looked after their children, and the focus on devoted motherhood was not so strong there.

The ideal German woman is one who puts her children before her career.

Motherhood

Much of a German woman's life revolves around her family. The modern German woman, especially if she has become a mother late in life, wants to enjoy a close relationship with her child. The paid maternity leave provided by law gives her a good start. Fathers are more willing to share in child care, unlike a few decades ago, when they would be teased as being a *Pantoffelheld* ("Pahn-TOH-fel-held," henpecked husband, literally slipper-hero).

Raven mothers Many Germans believe a woman should aim for a career if she is single, but when she becomes a mother, her motherhood role has priority. A mother who does not put her child before her career is called a "raven mother." (There is no apparent connection between the term and ravens.)

This attitude is reflected in the education system and the lack of infant care centers. Kindergartens open for fixed hours and normally close for lunch.

Schoolchildren only attend school when there are classes and in some states school may start and end at different times. If the last class is canceled for some reason, children go home. In addition, schoolchildren up to the 10th grade are sent home unannounced if the temperature in the shade at 10 a.m. exceeds 80.6°F. Not knowing when to expect a child home makes it difficult for most mothers to even think of part-time work outside the home.

Changing attitudes In the 1950s, most German women worked for a short while before getting married and stopped work even before the first child came. A woman who continued working was announcing to her neighbors that her husband was not earning enough to support the family. In the boom years of the 1960s, however, when labor was in short supply, about half a million women went to work.

In the 1970s, a "three-phase theory" for women was popular: first, school and job training, second, a family break of about 10–15 years, and third, back to work. During this time, thanks to the women's emancipation movement, it became acceptable for women to admit they wanted to work for personal satis-faction alone. In the 1980s, work became part of women's lifestyles.

There is a growing group of married women who have no choice in the matter. With a divorce rate of about 30%, marriage no longer means lifelong security. Pensions, too, have to be earned now, and the increasing number of poverty-stricken old women serves as a warning.

Day mothers Since childcare centers are so scarce, mothers who need time off approach other mothers or relatives to babysit. Few parents can afford a full-time nanny. Another alternative is the day-mother program borrowed from Sweden. In this program, children are looked after by qualified women who have passed stringent government conditions, including clean police and

A little girl plays "mother." What German society's attitude to motherhood and career women will be when she is old enough to choose, nobody can say.

A mother teaches her children how to cut a cake. In the background, hanging on the wall behind her head, are flowers being dried for decoration.

often means holding back a career, mothers stop work for an average of less than three years to look after children and try to keep close contact with their work place during the leave period. Many German women with more than one child stop work for an average of about seven years before going back to work, usually part-time. Some mothers continue to work after two months' maternity leave. Better educated women are more likely to believe in balancing family and work and less likely to give up their jobs for the family.

health records and knowledge of child education. As more mothers enter the labor force, there is a heavy demand for these women, and consequently a rapidly growing pool of day mothers who do not register with the government.

Modern mothers   The educated, modern woman demands greater help from her husband than before as she no longer wants to be a housewife all her life. Since giving up work for 10 years

Maternity benefits   Lower birth rates are disastrous to Germany's social security scheme since eventually there will be too few workers to support too many pensioners. This knowledge and the efforts of women leaders and trade unions have forced the government and businesses to help women balance work and family and make motherhood more attractive to them.

Protection for mothers

An expectant mother cannot be dismissed from her job until four months after childbirth. During a protective period starting six weeks before birth, she does not need to work unless she wishes to. For eight weeks after birth (12 for multiple births), work is prohibited. During this period, she receives a motherhood payment of between $2.50 and $16 dollars a day. If her pay is above this amount, say $20, her employer has to give her the difference. For companies with fewer than 30 employees, 80% of the amount is refunded by health insurance to lighten their burden. Other measures include the banning of strenuous work, time- or piece-rated work, work on weekends or at night, and work potentially dangerous to the expectant or nursing mother and her child.

Women have always been seen as "risk factors" in business because they may become mothers and either drop out of the work force or take extra leave for their children. In order to spread the risk factor more evenly, the law allows either parent, not only the mother, to take leave to look after a newborn baby for 18 months. During this time, if the parent does not work for more than 19 hours a week, a "salary" of 600 Deutschmarks (about $375) a month will be paid and the time credited in the pension calculations. The employee is protected from dismissal during this time. Housewives are also entitled to this payment and pension benefit as motherhood is recognized as a job.

Big business lends a hand Large businesses like IBM, Mercedes Benz, and Siemens have extended family breaks of two to seven years (sometimes more, where there are two or more children) to either parent. An equivalent job is guaranteed on return, but upgrading and refresher courses during the break period are pre-conditions. Smaller companies are not able to afford such generous concessions, making it difficult for the majority of mothers who work in such companies. The government is also making special efforts to help mothers get back to work through programs like subsidies, counseling, and skills-upgrading courses.

Single parenthood

The nuclear family (parents and their children) is still the tradition, but with an increasing divorce rate, many children are growing up with just one parent. In the former East Germany, only married couples were entitled to new housing, and those who married before 25 were given interest-free marriage loans. Having illegitimate children was not a disgrace. Single parent families were once labeled *Restfamilie* ("REST-fa-MI-li-eh," meaning partial family). The term is no longer used and Germans refer to the "one- or single-parent family."

In united Germany, more attention is being paid to the plight of single parents, many of whom are on welfare. Special assistance includes tax rebates, allowances for housing, child benefits, and cash advances where the father makes no payment. The law also recognizes the rights of illegitimate children to inheritance and support from their fathers.

Househusbands The modern young father is helping out more at home. Even advertisements feature athletic young fathers holding babies. Publicity is given to prominent and highly educated husbands of women politicians who stay home to look after the children and household while their wives make speeches in parliament. While the majority are still very conservative, an estimated 20,000 men in Germany now admit to being househusbands, marking a slow but sure trend that may accelerate in the 1990s.

A four-generation German family—the dream of many of Germany's senior citizens.

Growing old

Changing weather patterns have pushed fall and winter later into the year. For many Germans, mellowing into seniority, too, is taking place later through better medical care and financial well-being, as well as a new attitude of activity and vibrancy.

Germans call those above 60 the "older" generation and those above 75 the "old" generation or, in the former East Germany, "veterans." There is now a growing number of early retirees.

Women alone As a result of casualties in two world wars, there are twice as many women aged over 60 than men. Women also live longer than men, so the majority of older women are widows. The chances for remarriage are slim.

Multigeneration families are very rare now, so only 10% of older women live with their children under one roof. However, the ties between them are usually strong, and older women often help out where they can. Grandchildren give them a new lease of life. For the dual-career couple, having the children's grandmother babysit during the day is a boon.

Poverty in old age, especially for women, is a great problem in Germany. Most of these older women looked after homes and families all their lives, and have little or no pension to support them. Widows get only 60% of their husband's pension. Some who never married are poorly educated, had low-paying jobs, and consequently low pensions. Many of the old women are from the "Rubble Women" generation.

Women are the main recipients of social welfare benefits, but many more need welfare and do not apply through ignorance, shame, or fear that their children will be asked to contribute. Used to making sacrifices and doing without necessities, they accept their hardship and even manage to be energetic and cheerful.

Isolation In modern Germany, loneliness can also be a problem. Children often move to another town in search of work or to study, and even if they stay in town, they are often busy and have little time for their parents.

A woman widowed young, perhaps during the war, will have brought up her children alone, and in old age she will still be active and have a circle of friends. A woman widowed late, who has probably been a housewife all her life, is more likely to face problems of isolation.

Home nursing With growing age, family nursing becomes important. Women carry the main responsibility as most of this work is done by wives, daughters, and daughters-in-law. Whether for nursing women, their families, or the dependent relative, there is a heavy physical, emotional, and financial burden.

In rural areas, about one out of seven households nurses a sick family member at home. A woman may spend her life bringing up children and before she has time to enjoy her freedom, she has to nurse aged parents.

Homes for the aged About 80% of senior citizens in homes are women, many of whom feel neglected by their families and consider these homes a "waiting" station for death. Yet some elderly women now choose a suitable home before they actually need one.

An old age home is a costly alternative. For those who cannot afford one, the social welfare pays and asks their children to contribute. If the woman has a pension, she will only receive a small part of it and the rest is used to pay the home. Old people see these homes as a social and financial slide downward.

Elderly people today cling to their independence, preferring to live in their own home for as long as possible. They are sometimes supported by visiting nursing and medical help, qualified people who visit the homes of the elderly every day to look after their basic needs. "Meals on wheels" also help many elderly people lead independent and dignified lives.

The Gray Panthers

The women's movement of the 1960s and 1970s kindled an awareness in older women who had grown up in a traditional age. They changed their outlook, tried a new lifestyle, and tackled the problems of aging together. The best-known group of such women is called the Gray Panthers. It was founded by Trude Unruh in 1975, following the model founded by Maggie Kuhn in Philadelphia in 1970.

By 1987, there were about 170 groups of Gray Panthers all over Germany, with 150,000 members. Although they bear the same name, many work independently of each other. Through provocative and radical actions, they expose the shortcomings in old age homes and fight against leaving old people to the questionable mercy of institutions and the public.

Older people have been motivated to fight for their rights and needs, and to live a humane, self-determined, and meaningful life. Drastic situations where husbands and wives were forced to live separately are more history than fact today, partially through the efforts of the Gray Panthers.

The Gray Panthers have made the post-war "Rubble Women" a special cause. Today, these women are the grandmothers and great-grandmothers of Germany. Most have been

through marriages with husbands who were the absolute heads and breadwinners of the family. Many of them have nursed older relatives in multigeneration houses, but live alone today. Their tragedy is that they were not gainfully employed but unpaid housewives and mothers then, and poverty-stricken grandmothers today. Through the demonstrations and protests of the Gray Panthers, the "Rubble Women" have gained recognition of their contribution and sacrifices during the war.

Old fires and a new pride have been rekindled in Germany's senior citizens. They are now taking the advice they used to give their own children: If you want something, go out and get it yourself.

Swinging grandmas Thanks to an excellent health system, older women are able to stay active longer. They often go on health spa vacations paid for by public medical insurance and return feeling energized. This insurance program, which is compulsory, covers all medical and recuperative treatment, medicine, and hospitalization. Patients have to make a small contribution for medication and hospitalization in order to reduce Germany's escalating health costs.

Although many older women still have fulfilling roles within the family, they generally have more leisure time. There are countless activities aimed at giving them new interests; adult education courses, tours, hikes, historical and geographical programs, self-help groups like the "Old Helping Young" (where they offer their experience to help younger people), and dance afternoons are a few examples.

Charity and government institutions have also made greater efforts to help isolated women find a new interest in life. Unfortunately, few of those in poor health or from the lower working class are being reached.

As each generation grows older, there are more well-educated grandmothers who have not only benefited from better educational policies in the past decades, but who have also been touched by the feminist movement. They are more adventurous and younger at heart and in body than their mothers. Many of them zip around in their own cars and travel great distances to visit relatives or foreign countries. They also fill the seats of cultural and adult education programs. Growing old exuberantly, not gracefully, is their aim. The 21st century should bring a new generation of older German women who are no longer a venerable, ashen gray but a mix of vibrant colors and verve.

Above: Exercising in an old folks' home.

Opposite: Trude Unruh, founder of the Gray Panthers.

Women Firsts

Hanna Arendt	(1906–75) First woman to be granted a professorial chair at the University of Princeton. At 22, she obtained her doctorate in philosophy in Heidelberg. The Jewish sociologist and philosopher, who was born in Hanover, fled to America to escape the Nazis in 1933. In New York, she was politically active and lectured political science for many years. She was frequently honored and won many prizes for her work.
Anita Augsburg	(1857–1943) First German woman lawyer, a radical feminist who fought for women's rights. When she realized women needed a formal education to fight for their causes, she went to Zürich in Switzerland to study as women were not allowed to study in German colleges then. In 1897, at 40, she obtained a doctorate in law. The first woman to obtain a license to practice law in Germany was Maria Otto, who had to wait many years to be allowed to take the second and final exams in 1922 in spite of the fact that she had led the defense in hundreds of cases. The first lady judge was Dr. Maria Munk, who became assistant judge in 1924.
Cilly Aussem	The 21-year-old sports teacher from Cologne was the first German woman to win the coveted Wimbledon prize in 1930.
Elly Beinhorn-Rosemeyer	(b. 1907) First female pilot to win the Hindenburg Cup started in 1928 for the best pilot of the year. Her flight of more than 22,000 miles from Europe over Asia to Australia, South America and back lasted eight months, from December 4, 1931 to July 26, 1932.
Hrosvitha von Gandersheim	(935–973) First German dramatic poetess. She wrote her poems and dramas in Latin. Following her, Ava (d. 1127), a recluse and the first poetess in the German language, wrote *The Holy Story* in four spiritual poems.
Maria Göppert-Mayer	(1906–72) Joint winner of the 1963 Nobel Prize for Physics (together with J. Hans and D. Jensen for their discoveries on the nuclear shell structure, as well as with Eugene Eigner for his work on the theory of the atomic nucleus and the elementary particles). Born of a seven-generation family of college professors, she married and went to Baltimore with her American husband, Dr. Joseph Edward Mayer. She was dubbed "Madonna of the Onion" because of her description, in 1949, of the atomic nucleus: "Built up like an onion in layers with protons and neutrons revolving around each other and spinning in orbit like couples in a waltz around a ballroom."
Anna Louisa Karsch	(1722–91) A poor farm girl whose only lessons in reading and writing were given by her Great-uncle for four years till she was ten, yet she was the first woman to earn her living from writing. She had two unhappy marriages and seven children. To help supplement the family income, as her second husband was an alcoholic, she began writing poems and became famous a few years later, coming to the notice of the nobility, including Frederick II the Great. However, her life continued to be a difficult one as she had no steady income.
Margaretha Kirch	(1670–1720) One of the first German astronomers. Since a woman was not allowed to study astronomy, she published much of her work under her husband's name. In 1702, she discovered a comet. When her husband died, she was allowed to continue his work at the observatory in Guben.
Käthe Kruse	(b. 1883) She created the first life-like dolls because she disliked stiff, unnatural dolls, the only ones available for her children. Later, she made life-size dolls for window dressing.

Dorothea Leporin-Erxleben	(1715–62) First German woman to graduate as a medical doctor. In spite of heavy duties as a pastor's wife and stepmother to his four children, she managed to continue with her medical studies and practice. She was charged for practicing without a license. In 1754, she asked Frederick II the Great for permission to take the medical exams, which she passed with flying colors.
Nora Melle	(1899–1959) Co-founder and first chairwoman of the Information Service for Women Issues, now known as the German Women's Council. She organized the Council, the funding, and contacts with the media, as well as with politicians, and was chairwoman of the Council from 1951 to 1959.
Frederike Karoline Neuber	(1697–1760) One of the first of the great serious actresses of Germany. She ran away from a tyrannical father, married and joined a wandering comedy team at 20. Later, she became the director of a wandering theater. Influenced by the then "literature pope," Gottsched, she changed to a more serious style of acting, modelled along French theater lines, and replaced the popular improvised farces and harlequinades for carefully studied parts. This started a reform in German theater and raised the reputation of performers. A monument upon her death called her "the founder of good taste in the German theater."
Ida Noddack	(b. 1896) The chemist who discovered—together with her husband, Dr. Walter Noddack, and O.C. Berg—the chemical element rhenium in 1925. Working closely with her husband, she made many other discoveries, especially about radioactive material. Four years before it was confirmed by other scientists, she put forward the theory that uranium would disintegrate into larger parts if irradiated with neutrons.
Louise Otto-Peters	(1819–95) Together with other women, including Auguste Schmidt and Henriette Goldschmidt, she founded the General German Women's Association to fight for the rights of women in the first feminist movement of Germany.
Käthe Paulus	(1868–1935) First professional German airship pilot. In 1893, the 24-year-old woman jumped from the balloon *Adler* (*Eagle*) with her parachute. In 16 years, she went on 516 balloon flights and chalked up 147 jumps. In 1913–14, she invented the "parachute packet," a foldable parachute that played a great role in World War I and saved the lives of many balloonists and pilots.
Nelly Sachs	(1891–1970) First German poetess to win a Nobel Prize for literature.
Alice Salomon	(1872–1948) Founder of the first vocational social work school for women. Although she did not have a college degree, she obtained a doctorate in philosophy from the University of Berlin because of a brilliantly written thesis. She was active in the German women's movement and the International Women's Association in London, becoming its vice-president in 1932. As a Jew, she was forced into exile by the Nazis in 1937 and her name was not allowed to be mentioned. Her books on women's issues, economics and education are still highly respected and valid today.
Elisabeth Schwarzhaupt	(1901–86) First female federal minister, she was put in charge of the health department from 1961 to 1966 through two government periods.
Hildegard Wegscheider	(1871–1953) First woman in Prussia to obtain the pre-college degree and a doctorate in philosophy. She was not allowed into the University of Berlin and had to go to Halle instead. For her later work in women's education, rights, and political work, she was one of the first women to be granted a Federal Cross of Merit.
Mary Wigmann	(1886–1973) Pioneer of modern expressionist dance. Many of her students became famous and she was celebrated even in the United States.

Glossary

Note: A German noun begins with a capital letter.

au pair Tutoring post, usually only for a young woman, that includes housework and babysitting, enabling her to learn the local language at the same time.

Beginen ("bay-GI-nen") In the Middle Ages, women who did not take the church oath as nuns did, but lived in convents or Beginen houses donated by rich people.

capitalism Economic system with private or corporate ownership of capital. Prices, production, and distribution of goods are determined by the free market.

communism A classless social and political system where the people or the state owns and controls the means of production, and wealth is divided according to each person's need.

Deutsch ("DOY-tch") German.

Deutschland Germany, a federation of 16 states. Some parties in the opposition in the federal parliament govern some states. Although there is a national constitution, each state has its own laws for the police, environment, schools, cultural programs, and administration, among other things.

Deutschmark German currency.

fascism Political system exercising severe dictatorial control.

Germanic Adjective describing Indo-European tribes who lived in central and northern Europe and their customs. The Germans descended from the Franks, Thuringians, Saxons, Swabians, Alemans, and Bavarians.

German states There are 16 states or *Länder* making up the old German states (formerly West Germany, now Old Federal States) and the new German states (formerly East Germany, now New Federal States). The old states include Schleswig Holstein, Hamburg, Lower Saxony, Saar, and Bavaria. New states include Brandenburg and Saxony.

Gulash Spicy stew or soup with meat and onions, using paprika as a spice.

Hausfrau ("HOUSE-frao") Housewife.

Nazis Members of the former National Socialist German Workers' Party founded on fascist principles in 1919 and headed by Hitler from 1921. They were extremely racialistic and anti-Semitic, murdering millions of Jews, gypsies, and others. Their policies reduced women to domestic duties and being birth-givers.

political parties *Social Democratic Party* (SPD), traditionally a workers' party, the first one to fight for women's rights. SPD chancellors: Willy Brandt (1969–74), Helmut Schmidt (1974–82). The ruling *Christian Democratic Party* (CDU) and *Christian Socialist Union* (CSU) in Bavaria are conservative parties. CDU chancellors: Konrad Adenauer (1949–63), Ludwig Erhard (1963–66), Kurt Kiesinger (1966–69), Helmut Kohl (1987–). The CDU's coalition partner is the *Free Democratic Party* (FDP). The *Green party* is an ecological party with the greatest female participation. (Party abbreviations are of their German names.)

Prussia German kingdom with Berlin as its capital. It became a military power in the 18th and 19th centuries and united Germany and Western Poland. After World War II, it was abolished and reorganized by Britain, the United States, France, and Russia, and parts of it came under Russian and Polish administration.

raven mothers From the German *Raben Mutter*, a term censuring mothers who neglect their children.

Reichstag ("RAI-sh-tahg") German parliament until 1945.

revolution Great social change or upheaval, usually by force.

social democracy Political principle of the gradual and peaceful transition from capitalism to socialism by democratic means.

Further Reading

Barrell, Brigitte and Fison, Brent: *Another Bridge*, Far Hills Publishing, Buffalo, NY, 1992.

Fout, John C.: *German Women in the 19th Century*, Holmes and Meier, New York, 1984.

Joeres, Ruth-Ellen and Maynes, Mary Jo: *German Women in the 18th and 19th Century: A Social and Literary History*, Indiana University Press, Bloomington, Indiana, 1986.

Koonz, Claudia: *Mothers in the Fatherland: Women, the Family, and Nazi Politics*, St. Martin's Press, New York, 1988.

Philipsen, Dirk: *We Were the People: Voices from East Germany's Revolutionary Autumn of 1989*, Duke University Press, Durham, NC, 1992.

Poewe, Karla: *Childhood in Germany During World War II: The Story of a Little Girl*, E. Mellen, Lewiston, NY, 1992.

Weeden, Chris (editor): *Die Frau in der DDR: An Anthology of Women's Writing from the German Democratic Republic*, Blackwell Publications, Cambridge, MA, 1988.

Index

abortion laws, demonstration against 29–30
Ackermann, Dr. Lea 52
"alibi" women 39–40
apprenticeship 18–19, 38–39, 110
aristocratic women 17
Association of German Women Doctors 45
Augsburg, Anita 42, 124

Bausch, Pina 61
Bebel, August 25
Beginen homes 15, 126
Bingen, Hildegard von 14
birth customs 12–13, 103–105
Bora, Katarina von 16
Brahms, Johannes 8–9
Braun, Lily 22–23
business management 39–42

child care 31, 116–119
Christian ceremonies 104, 106
Christian Democratic Union 48–49
Christian Socialist Union 49
Christianity 14–16
church reform 16
composers, women 9, 59

dancers 60–61
Dierks, Johanna 44
Dietrich, Marlene 100–101
Doenhoff, Marion 55

Doerrie, Dorris 63
Dohm, Hedwig 23, 89
Droste-Huelshoff, Annette 56–57
drug abuse in sports 64

East German women 32–34, 49
education 14–15, 16, 23, 33, 86, 90, 109–111
    of minorities 68–69, 71, 76, 77, 79–80
Einsele, Dr. Helga 53
emancipators 22–25, 86–94
Emma 29, 54
Emmerich, Dr. Erica 40
entrepreneurs 40–41

Falck, Dr. Ingeborg 45
farming 12
Federation of German Women's Associations 25, 27, 86
Federation of Socialist German Students 29
Fichtel, Anja 65
Firch, Franziska 38
Free Democratic Party 48–49, 86, 88
French Revolution 21, 59

Gandersheim, Hrosvitha von 14, 124
General German Women's Association 23, 25, 89–90, 92
German Communist Party 94, 96
German resettlers 67–69

German Women Jurists Association 43–44
German Women's Council 28, 34, 125
Germanic tribes and customs 11–14
Gisela, Princess of Saxony 17
Graf, Steffi 65
Gray Panthers 122
Greek women 81
Green party 47–49
Greenpeace 97–98
Griefahn, Monika 97–99
guest workers 73
guilds 18–19
Guillaume-Schack, Gertrude 25
gypsy women 26, 70–72

Hartmann, Fatima 3
Hasselblatt-Diedrich, Dr. Ingrid 46
Heuser-Schreiber, Dr. Hedda 46
Hildebrandt, Regine 49
Hitler, Adolf 26–28
home industry 20, 25

Ihrer, Emma 50
Industrial Revolution 22
Italian women 79–82

Jews 26
Juhacz, Maria 95–96

Kelley, Petra 47
Kirchner, Johanna 95–96

Kirsch, Sarah 58
Kuczynski, Rita 58

Lange, Helene 23, 86, 89–90
language learning 68, 73
law, women in 42–44
laws helping women 31, 88, 118–119
literary salons 21
literature 56–58
literature, socialist 58
Lueders, Marie-Elisabeth 26, 86–88
Luther, Martin 16
Luxemburg, Rosa 24, 94

marriage 12, 22, 33–34, 91–92, 113–115
    gypsies 71
    Italians 80
    Moslems 75
media, women in the 54–55
medicine, women in 44–46
Middle Ages 17–20, 56, 105
middle-class women 22, 94
minorities 67–81
    generation problems of 73–74
monogamy 14
Morgner, Irmtraud 58
Moslems 75–77
motherhood 26, 33, 50, 116–119
mothers
    day mothers 117–118
    raven mothers 40, 116, 126
    recuperation of 52
    unwed 15, 119
    working 40, 116–118
movements, women's 22–25, 28–29
movie production 62
Munk, Maria 42, 124
music, women in 7–9, 59–60
Mutter, Anne-Sophie 60

Nadig, Friederike 31
Nazis 26–27, 42, 57, 71, 88, 94–96, 126
networking of businesswomen 42
Niemeyer, Gisela 43
Noelle-Neumann, Elizabeth 41
nuns 14–16, 18, 52, 83–86

old age 120–123
Otto-Peters, Louise 22–23, 91–92, 125

Palucca, Gret 61
peasants 18
Peschel-Gutzeit, Maria 43
Pfau, Dr. Ruth 83–86
political parties, perception of women 49
politics, women in 47–49, 86–99

priestesses 11–8
property, women and 12

queens 17–18
quotas 31, 48, 50
religion
    of gypsies 71
    of Turks 75
resistance fighters 27, 95–96
Retzlaff, Dr. Ingeborg 45
Riefenstahl, Leni 63
Rosh, Lea 55
"Rubble Women" 28, 31, 45
Russians 69

Sachs, Nelly 56–57, 125
Salomon, Alice 53, 125
Sander, Jil 41
Scheinhardt, Dr. Saliha 76
Scholl, Sophie 27
Schumann, Clara 6–9
Schumann, Robert 7–9
Schwarz, Sybilla 56
Schwarzer, Alice 29, 54, 56
Schwarzhaupt, Dr. Elisabeth 48, 88, 125
Seghers, Anna 56
Selbert, Elisabeth 31
Social Democratic Party 24, 25, 48–49, 94–96, 126
socialist movement 25, 93–94
spinning 18
sports, women in 64–65
Stefan, Verena 56
Suessmuth, Rita 48–9

technical work 37–39
teenagers 107–108
    Turkish 75
Thusnelda 13
trade unions, women in 50–51
Trotta, Margarethe von 62–63
Turkish women 75–77

unity, German 35
Unruh, Trude 122

Varnhagen von Ense, Rahel 21
Veleda the Virgin 12
virtue of women 12, 71, 75
Vollmer, Antje 47
vote, women and the 26

Wander, Maxie 58
wars 11, 19, 26–27
Weber, Helene 31
wedding customs 113–115

welfare work, women in 52–53
Wesel, Helen 31
Wieck, Frederick 7
Wigmann, Mary 60–61, 125
witches 15–16
Wolf, Christa 58
work bans on women 19, 26, 31, 38–3, 50
work, inequality at 32–34, 50, 112–113
Working Women's Association 25
working-class women 25, 93–94
World War I 26
World War II 26–28, 42
writers, women 14, 54–58, 76, 91–92, 94
Wulf-Mathies, Monika 51

Yugoslavian women 78–79

Zechlin, Ruth 59–60
Zetkin, Clara 24, 91, 93–94

Picture Credits